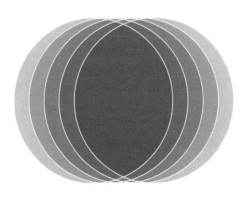

FIVE
TOWARDS
A DEEPER EXPERIENCE
OF GOD'S GRACE

POINTS

JOHN PIPER

CHRISTIAN
FOCUS

© The Desiring God Foundation 2013
paperback ISBN 978-1-78191-252-2
epub ISBN 978-1-78191-284-3
Mobi ISBN 978-1-78191-285-0

10 9 8 7 6 5 4 3 2 1

Published in 2013

by

Christian Focus Publications Ltd.,
Geanies House, Fearn, Ross-shire,
IV20 1TW, Scotland, Great Britain
www.christianfocus.com
www.desiringGod.org

Cover design by DUFI-ART.com
Printed and bound in the USA

CONTENTS

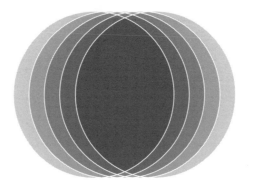

FIVE
POINTS

1
PREFACE

Christians love God. He is our great Treasure, and nothing can compare with him. One of the great old catechisms says, "God is a Spirit, infinite, eternal, and unchangeable, in his being, wisdom, power, holiness, justice, goodness, and truth."[1] This is the One we love. We love the whole panorama of his perfections. To know him, and be loved by him, and become like him is the end of our soul's quest. He is our "exceeding joy" (Ps. 43:4).

He is infinite—and that answers our longing for completeness. He is eternal—and that answers our longing for permanence. He is unchangeable—and that answers our longing for stability and security. There is none like God. Nothing can compare with him. Wealth, sex, power, popularity, conquest, productivity, great achievement—nothing can compare with God.

When the Fog Clears
The more you know him, the more you want to know him. The more you feast on his fellowship, the hungrier you are for deeper, richer communion. Satisfaction at the deepest levels

---

1   Westminster Shorter Catechism, Question Four.

breeds a holy longing for the time when we will have the very power of God to love God.

That's the way Jesus prays for us to his Father: "That the love with which you have loved me may be in them" (John 17:26). That is what we long for: the very love the Father has for the Son filling us, enabling us to love the Son with the magnitude and purity of the love of the Father. Then the frustrations of inadequate love will be over.

Yes, the more you know him and love him and trust him, the more you long to know him. That's why I have written this little book. I long to know God and enjoy God. And I want the same for you. The great old catechism asks, "What is the chief end of man?" and answers, "Man's chief end is to glorify God and *enjoy* him forever."[2] Enjoying God is the way to glorify God, because *God is most glorified in us when we are most satisfied in him.*

But to enjoy him we must know him. Seeing is savoring. If he remains a blurry, vague fog, we may be intrigued for a season. But we will not be stunned with joy, as when the fog clears and you find yourself on the brink of some vast precipice.

Worthwhile Wrestling

My experience is that clear knowledge of God from the Bible is the kindling that sustains the fires of affection for God. And probably the most crucial kind of knowledge is the knowledge of what God is like in salvation. That is what the five points of Calvinism are about. Not the power and sovereignty of God in general, but his power and sovereignty in the way he saves people. That is why these points are sometimes called *the doctrines of grace.* To experience God fully, we need to know not just how he acts in general, but specifically how he saves *us*—how did he save me?

---

2   Westminster Shorter Catechism, Question One.

I do not begin as a Calvinist and defend a system. I begin as a Bible-believing Christian who wants to put the Bible above all systems of thought. But over the years—many years of struggle—I have deepened in my conviction that Calvinistic teachings on the five points are biblical and therefore true, and therefore a precious pathway into deeper experiences of God's grace.

My own struggle makes me more patient with others who are on the way. And in one sense, we are all on the way. Even when we know things biblically and truly—things clear enough and precious enough to die for—we still see through a glass dimly (1 Cor. 13:12). There can be many tears as we seek to put our ideas through the testing fires of God's word.

But all the wrestling to understand what the Bible teaches about God is worth it. God is a rock of strength in a world of quicksand. To know him in his sovereignty is to become like an oak tree in the wind of adversity and confusion. And along with strength is sweetness and tenderness beyond imagination. The sovereign Lion of Judah is the sweet Lamb of God.

My Prayer for You

I pray you will be helped. Please don't feel that you have to read these short chapters in any particular order. Many of you will want to skip the historical introduction because it is not as immediately relevant to the biblical questions. There is an intentional order to the book, but feel free to start wherever it looks most urgent for you. If you get help, then you will be drawn back to the rest of it. If you don't, well, then just return to the Bible and read it with all your might. That is where I hope you will end up anyway: reading and understanding and loving and enjoying and obeying God's word, not my word. I pray that because of our meeting here you will move "Towards a Deeper Experience of God's Grace."

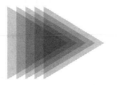

2
HISTORICAL ROOTS

John Calvin, the famous theologian and pastor of Geneva, died in 1564. Along with Martin Luther in Germany, he was the most influential force of the Protestant Reformation. His commentaries and *Institutes of the Christian Religion* are still exerting tremendous influence on the Christian church worldwide.

The churches which have inherited the teachings of Calvin are usually called Reformed as opposed to the Lutheran or Anglican/Episcopalian branches of the Reformation. While not all Baptist churches hold to a Reformed theology, there is a significant Baptist tradition which flowed out of that stream and still cherishes the central doctrines inherited from the Reformed branch of the Reformation.

Arminius and the Remonstrants
The controversy between Arminianism and Calvinism arose in Holland in the early 1600s. The founder of the Arminian party was Jacob Arminius (1560–1609). He studied in Geneva under Calvin's successor, Theodore Beza, and became a professor of theology at the University of Leyden in 1603.

Gradually Arminius came to reject certain Calvinist teachings. The controversy spread all over Holland, where the Reformed

Church was the overwhelming majority. The Arminians drew up their creed in Five Articles, and laid them before the state authorities of Holland in 1610 under the name Remonstrance, signed by forty-six ministers.

The official Calvinistic response came from the Synod of Dort which was held November 13, 1618, to May 9, 1619, to consider the Five Articles. There were eighty-four members and eighteen secular commissioners. The Synod wrote what has come to be known as the Canons of Dort. These are still part of the church confession of the Reformed Church in America and the Christian Reformed Church. They state the Five Points of Calvinism in response to the Five Articles of the Arminian Remonstrants.

So the so-called Five Points were not chosen by the Calvinists as a summary of their teaching. They emerged as a response to the Arminians who chose these five points to disagree with.

At the Heart of Biblical Theology
It is more important to give a positive biblical position on the five points than to know the exact form of the original controversy. These five points are still at the heart of biblical theology. They are not unimportant. Where we stand on these things deeply affects our view of God, man, salvation, the atonement, regeneration, assurance, worship, and missions.

Somewhere along the way (nobody knows for sure when or how), the five points came to be summarized in English under the acronym TULIP.

> T – Total depravity
> U – Unconditional election
> L – Limited atonement
> I – Irresistible grace
> P – Perseverance of the saints

I make no claim that these five points exhaust the riches of Reformed theology. Numerous writers, especially those with a more Presbyterian orientation, make that point today because so many people (like me, a Baptist) are called Calvinists while not embracing all aspects of the Reformed tradition. For example, Richard Muller in his book, *Calvin and the Reformed Tradition,*[1] and Kenneth J. Stewart in *Ten Myths About Calvinism*[2] make clear that Calvin and the system of rivers that flowed from his labors are wider and deeper and more multi-faceted than the five streams I am focusing on here. These five points are focused on the central act of God's saving sinners. Nor do I make the claim that these titles for the five doctrines of grace are the best titles. Like any shorthand version of a doctrine, they are all liable to misunderstanding. Justin Taylor gives a helpful summary of various attempts to restate these truths.[3]

For example, Timothy George prefers R O S E S over T U L I P: Radical depravity, Overcoming grace, Sovereign election, Eternal life, Singular redemption. Roger Nicole prefers the acronym G O S P E L (which makes six points): Grace, Obligatory grace, Sovereign grace, Provision-making grace, Effectual grace, Lasting grace.

Others abandon the effort to make an acronym altogether. For example, James Montgomery Boice suggests: Radical depravity, Unconditional election, Particular redemption, Efficacious grace, Persevering grace. Greg Forster proposes:

- State of man before salvation: wholly defiled
- Work of the Father in salvation: unconditional choice

---

1   Richard Muller, *Calvin and the Reformed Tradition* (Grand Rapids: Baker Books, 2012), pp. 51-69.

2   Kenneth J. Stewart, *Ten Myths About Calvinism* (Downers Grove, Illinois: Inter-Varsity Press, 2011), pp. 75-96.

3   http://thegospelcoalition.org/blogs/justintaylor/2011/11/08/tweaking-the-tulip/ (accessed 5-29-2013).

- Work of the Son in salvation: personal salvation
- Work of the Spirit in salvation: supernatural transformation
- State of man after salvation: in faith, perseverance

Nor do I claim that this ordering of the doctrines (T U L I P) is necessarily the most helpful when teaching what they mean. To be sure, there is a good rationale for this traditional order. It starts with man in need of salvation (Total depravity) and then gives, in the order of their occurrence, the steps God takes to save his people. He elects (Unconditional election), then he sends Jesus to atone for the sins of the elect (Limited atonement), then he irresistibly draws his people to faith (Irresistible grace), and finally works to cause them to persevere to the end (Perseverance of the saints).

I have found, however, that people grasp these points more easily if we go in the order in which we ourselves often experience them when we become Christians.

1. We experience first our depravity and need of salvation.
2. Then we experience the irresistible grace of God leading us toward faith.
3. Then we trust the sufficiency of the atoning death of Christ for our sins.
4. Then we discover that behind the work of God to atone for our sins and bring us to faith was the unconditional election of God.
5. And finally we rest in his electing grace to give us the strength and will to persevere to the end in faith.

This is the order we follow in the pages ahead. I will try to lay out what I believe the Scriptures teach on these five points. My great desire is to deepen your experience of God's grace and to honor him by understanding and believing his truth revealed in Scripture.

I pray that I am open to changing any of my ideas which can be shown to contradict the truth of Scripture. I do not have any vested interest in John Calvin himself, and find some of what he taught to be wrong. But in general I am willing to be called a Calvinist on the five points because this name has been attached to these points for centuries and because I find this Calvinist position to be faithful to Scripture. The Bible is our final authority.

I share the sentiments of Jonathan Edwards who said in the preface to his great book *The Freedom of the Will*, "I should not take it at all amiss, to be called a Calvinist, for distinction's sake: though I utterly disclaim a dependence on Calvin, or believing the doctrines which I hold, because he believed and taught them; and cannot justly be charged with believing in every thing just as he taught."[4]

It might be helpful for some readers to summarize the meaning of each of the five points briefly before we go into more biblical detail. Perhaps this foretaste will awaken some sense of why I believe these truths magnify God's precious grace and give unspeakable joy to sinners who have despaired of saving themselves.

Total Depravity

Our sinful corruption is so deep and so strong as to make us slaves of sin and morally unable to overcome our own rebellion and blindness. This inability to save ourselves from ourselves is *total*. We are utterly dependent on God's grace to overcome our rebellion, give us eyes to see, and effectively draw us to the Savior.

Unconditional Election

God's election is an unconditional act of free grace that was given through his Son Jesus before the world began. By this act, God chose, before the foundation of the world, those who would

---

4   *The Freedom of the Will* (1754), ed. Paul Ramsey (New Haven, Conn. Yale University Press, 1957), p. 131.

be delivered from bondage to sin and brought to repentance and saving faith in Jesus.

Limited Atonement

The atonement of Christ is *sufficient* for all humans and *effective* for those who trust him. It is not limited in its worth or sufficiency to save all who believe. But the *full, saving effectiveness* of the atonement that Jesus accomplished is limited to those for whom that saving effect was prepared. The availability of the total sufficiency of the atonement is for all people. Whosoever will— whoever believes—will be covered by the blood of Christ. *And* there is a divine design in the death of Christ to accomplish the promises of the new covenant for the chosen bride of Christ. Thus Christ died for all people, but not for all in the same way.

Irresistible Grace

This means that the resistance that all human beings exert against God every day (Rom. 3:10-12; Acts 7:51) is wonderfully overcome at the proper time by God's saving grace for undeserving rebels whom he chooses freely to save.

Perseverance of the Saints

We believe that all who are justified will win the fight of faith. They will persevere in faith and will not surrender finally to the enemy of their souls. This perseverance is the promise of the new covenant, obtained by the blood of Christ, and worked in us by God himself, yet not so as to diminish, but only to empower and encourage, our vigilance; so that we may say in the end, *I have fought the good fight, but it was not I, but the grace of God which was with me* (2 Tim. 4:7; 1 Cor. 15:10).

We turn now to give a biblical explanation and justification for each of the five points. I pray not that I will be proved right, but that the word of God will be truly explained and our minds would be softened to receive what is really there.

3
TOTAL DEPRAVITY

When we speak of man's depravity, we mean man's natural condition apart from any grace exerted by God to restrain or transform man.

The totality of that depravity is clearly not that man does as much evil as he could do. There is no doubt that man could perform more evil acts toward his fellow man than he does. But if he is restrained from performing more evil acts by motives that are not owing to his glad submission to God, then even his "virtue" is evil in the sight of God. Romans 14:23 says, "Whatever does not proceed from faith is sin."[1] This is a radical

---

[1] I agree with Thomas Schreiner that this verse is introduced precisely because it stands as a sweeping maxim with profound biblical warrant: Acting without faith is sinning. "Thus Augustine (*On the Proceedings of Pelagius* 34; *On the Grace of Christ* 1.27; *On Marriage and Concupiscence* 1.4; *Against Two Letters of the Pelagians* 1.7; 3.14; *On the Predestination of the Saints* 20) was right in claiming that any act done apart from faith is sin." *Romans*, Baker Exegetical Commentary on the New Testament, Vol. 6 (Grand Rapids, MI: Baker, 1998), p. 739. Schreiner points out that Paul could very easily have made a more limited point by stopping with the first part of verse 23 ("But whoever has doubts is condemned if he eats, because the eating is not from faith"), but when he adds the unqualified maxim, "For whatever does not proceed from faith is sin," he broadens the foundation to a general statement. Schreiner also points to the fact that in Romans 4:18-21, we see why this is so—namely, that acting in faith glorifies God, and we are to do that in every detail of life (1 Cor. 10:31). Not relying on God in any action or thought takes power and glory to ourselves (1 Pet. 4:11; 1 Cor. 15:10; Gal. 2:20). That is sin, even if the external deed itself accords with God's will.

indictment of all natural "virtue" that does not flow from a heart humbly relying on God's grace.

An example might make this radical indictment of much human "goodness" clearer. Suppose you're the father of a teenage son. You remind him to wash the car before he uses it to take his friends to the basketball game tonight. He had earlier agreed to do that. He gets angry and says he doesn't want to. You gently but firmly remind him of his promise and say that's what you expect. He resists. You say, Well, if you are going to use the car tonight, that's what you agreed to do. He storms out of the room angry. Later you see him washing the car. But he is not doing it out of love for you or out of a Christ-honoring desire to honor you as his father. He wants to go to the game with his friends. That is what constrains his "obedience." I put "obedience" in quotes because it is only external. His heart is wrong. This is what I mean when I say that all human "virtue" is depraved if it is not from a heart of love to the heavenly Father—even if the behavior conforms to biblical norms.

The terrible condition of man's heart will never be recognized by people who assess it only in relation to other men. Your son will drive his friends to the ballgame. That is "kindness," and they will experience it as a benefit. So the evil of our actions can never be measured merely by the harm they do to other humans. Romans 14:23 makes plain that depravity is our condition in relation to God primarily, and only secondarily in relation to man. Unless we start here, we will never grasp the totality of our natural depravity.

Man's depravity is total in at least four senses.

1. Our rebellion against God is total.
Apart from the grace of God, there is no delight in the holiness of God, and there is no glad submission to the sovereign authority of God.

Of course, totally depraved men can be very religious and very philanthropic. They can pray and give alms and fast, as Jesus said (Matt. 6:1-18). But their very religion is rebellion against the rights of their Creator, if it does not come from a childlike heart of trust in the free grace of God. Religion is one of the chief ways that man conceals his unwillingness to forsake self-reliance and bank all his hopes on the unmerited mercy of God (Luke 18:9-14; Col. 2:20-23).

The totality of our rebellion is seen in Romans 3:9-11 and 18. "We have already charged that all, both Jews and Greeks, are under sin, as it is written: 'None is righteous, no, not one; no one understands; no one seeks for God.' ... 'There is no fear of God before their eyes.'" Any seeking of God that honors God is a gift of God. It is not owing to our native goodness. It is an illustration of God mercifully overcoming our native resistance to God.

Natural Man Not Seeking God

It is a myth that man in his natural state is genuinely seeking God. Men do seek God. But they do not seek him for who he is. They seek him in a pinch as one who might preserve them from death or enhance their worldly enjoyments. Apart from conversion, no one comes to the light of God.

Some do come to the light. But listen to what John 3:20-21 says about them. "Everyone who does wicked things hates the light and does not come to the light, lest his works should be exposed. But whoever does what is true comes to the light, so that it may be clearly seen that his works have been carried out in God." Yes, there are those who come to the light—namely, those whose deeds are the work of God. "Carried out in (or by) God" means worked by God. Apart from this gracious work of God all men hate the light of God and will not come to him lest their evil be exposed—this is total rebellion. "No one seeks for God.... There is no fear of God before their eyes!"

2. In his total rebellion everything man does is sin.

In Romans 14:23 Paul says, "Whatever does not proceed from faith is sin." Therefore, if all men are in total rebellion, everything they do is the product of rebellion and cannot be an honor to God, but only part of their sinful rebellion. Of course many of these acts which flow from inward unbelief conform outwardly to the revealed will of God (for example, obeying parents or telling the truth). But they do not conform to God's perfect will because of that mere outward conformity. Let all things be done in love, the apostle says (1 Cor. 16:14); but love is the fruit of faith (Gal. 5:6; 1 Tim. 1:5). Therefore many outwardly good acts come from hearts without Christ-exalting faith, and therefore, without love, and therefore without conformity to God's command, and therefore are sinful.

If a king teaches his subjects how to fight well and then those subjects rebel against their king and use the very skill he taught them to resist him, then even those skills, as excellent and amazing and "good" as they are, become evil.

Thus man does many things which he can do only because he is created in the image of God and which in the service of God would be praised. But in the service of man's self-justifying rebellion, these very things are sinful. We may praise them as echoes of God's excellence, but we will weep that they are prostituted for God-ignoring purposes.

In Romans 7:18 Paul says, "I know that nothing good dwells in me, that is, in my flesh." This is a radical confession of the truth that in our rebellion nothing we think or feel is good. It is all part of our rebellion. The fact that Paul qualifies his depravity with the words, "that is, in my flesh," shows that he is willing to affirm the good of anything that the Spirit of God produces in him (Rom. 15:18). "Flesh" refers to man in his natural state apart from the work of God's Spirit. So, what Paul is saying in Romans 7:18 is that apart from the work of God's Spirit all we think and feel and do is not good.

The Good That Really Counts
We recognize that the word "good" has a broad range of meanings. We will have to use it in a restricted sense to refer to many actions of fallen people which in relation to God are in fact not good.

For example, we will have to say that it is good that most unbelievers do not kill and that many unbelievers perform acts of benevolence. What we mean when we call such actions good is that they more or less conform to the external pattern of life that God has commanded in Scripture.

However, such outward conformity to the revealed will of God is not righteousness in relation to God. It is not done out of reliance on him or for his glory. He is not trusted for the resources, though he gives them all. Nor is his honor exalted, even though that's his will in all things (1 Cor. 10:31). Therefore even these "good" acts are part of our rebellion and are not "good" in the sense that really counts in the end—in relation to God.

3. Man's inability to submit to God and do good is total.
Picking up on the term "flesh" above (man apart from the grace of God), we find Paul declaring it to be totally enslaved to rebellion. Romans 8:7-8 says, "The mind that is set on the flesh is hostile to God, for it does not submit to God's law; indeed, it cannot. Those who are in the flesh cannot please God."

The "mind that is set on the flesh" (literally, "mind of the flesh") is the mind of man apart from the indwelling Spirit of God ("You, however, are not in the flesh but in the Spirit, if in fact the Spirit of God dwells in you," Romans 8:9). So natural man has a mindset that does not and cannot submit to God. Man cannot reform himself.

Ephesians 2:1 says that we Christians were all once "dead in trespasses and sins." The point of deadness is that we were incapable of any spiritual life with God. We had physical life, but our hearts were like a stone toward God (Eph. 4:18; Ezek. 36:26). Our hearts were blind and incapable of seeing the glory of God in Christ (2 Cor. 4:4-6). We were totally unable to reform ourselves.

4. Our rebellion is totally deserving of eternal punishment.
Ephesians 2:3 goes on to say that in our deadness we were "children of wrath." That is, we were under God's wrath because of the corruption of our hearts that made us as good as dead before God.

The reality of hell is God's clear indictment of the infiniteness of our guilt. If our corruption were not deserving of an eternal punishment, God would be unjust to threaten us with a punishment so severe as eternal torment. But the Scriptures teach that God is just in condemning unbelievers to eternal hell (2 Thess. 1:6-9; Matt. 5:29-30; 10:28; 13:49-50; 18:8-9; 25:46; Rev. 14:9-11; 20:10). Therefore, to the extent that hell is a sentence of total condemnation, to that extent must we think of ourselves as totally blameworthy apart from the saving grace of God.

This Terrible Truth of Total Depravity
In summary, total depravity means that our rebellion against God is total, everything we do in this rebellion is sinful, our inability to submit to God or reform ourselves is total, and we are therefore totally deserving of eternal punishment.

It is hard to exaggerate the importance of admitting our condition to be this bad. If we think of ourselves as basically good or even less than totally at odds with God, our grasp of the work of God in redemption will be defective. But if we humble ourselves under this terrible truth of our total depravity, we will be in a position to see and appreciate the glory and wonder of the work of God discussed in the next four points.

The aim of this book is to deepen our experience of God's grace. The aim is not to depress or to discourage or to paralyze. Knowing the seriousness of our disease will make us all the more amazed at the greatness of our Physician. Knowing the extent of our deep-seated rebellion will stun us at the long-suffering grace and patience of God toward us. The way we worship God and the way we treat other people, especially our enemies, are profoundly and wonderfully affected by knowing our depravity to the full.

4
IRRESISTIBLE GRACE

You will notice that I am changing the traditional order of T U L I P. The I stands for irresistible grace and usually comes fourth. I am putting it second after the T which stands for total depravity. The reason is that over the years my experience has been that most Christians have a conscious, personal experience of irresistible grace, even if they have never called it that. This personal experience of the reality of irresistible grace helps people grasp more quickly what these five points are all about. This in turn opens them to the biblical truthfulness of the other points.

More specifically, I rarely meet Christians who want to take credit for their conversion. There is something about true grace in the believer's heart that makes us want to give all the glory to God. So, for example, if I ask a believer how he will answer Jesus's question at the last judgment, "Why did you believe on me, when you heard the gospel, but your friends didn't, when they heard it?" very few believers answer that question by saying: "Because I was wiser or smarter or more spiritual or better trained or more humble." Most of us feel instinctively that we should glorify God's grace by saying: "There but for the grace of God go I." In other words, we know intuitively that God's grace was decisive in our conversion. That is what we mean by irresistible grace.

But We Do Resist Grace

The doctrine of irresistible grace does not mean that every influence of the Holy Spirit cannot be resisted. It means that the Holy Spirit, whenever he chooses, can overcome all resistance and make his influence irresistible.

In Acts 7:51 Stephen says to the Jewish leaders, "You stiff-necked people, uncircumcised in heart and ears, you always resist the Holy Spirit. As your fathers did, so do you." And Paul speaks of grieving and quenching the Holy Spirit (Eph. 4:30; 1 Thess. 5:19). God gives many entreaties and promptings which are resisted. In fact, the whole history of Israel in the Old Testament is one protracted story of human resistance to God's commands and promises, as the parable of the wicked tenants shows (Matt. 21:33-43; cf. Rom. 10:21). This resistance does not contradict God's sovereignty. God allows it, and overcomes it whenever he chooses.

The doctrine of irresistible grace means that God is sovereign and can conquer all resistance when he wills. "He does according to his will in the host of heaven and among the inhabitants of the earth; and none can stay his hand!" (Dan. 4:35). "Our God is in the heavens; he does all that he pleases" (Ps. 115:3). When God undertakes to fulfill his sovereign purpose, no one can successfully resist him. "I know that you can do all things, and that no purpose of yours can be thwarted" (Job 42:2).

God's Work of Bringing Us to Faith

This is what Paul taught in Romans 9:14-18, which caused his opponent to say, "Why then does he still find fault? For who can resist his will?" To which Paul answers: "Who are you, O man, to answer back to God? Will what is molded say to its molder, 'Why have you made me like this?' Has the potter no right over the clay, to make out of the same lump one vessel for honorable use and another for dishonorable use?" (Rom. 9:20-21).

More specifically, irresistible grace refers to the sovereign work of God to overcome the rebellion of our heart and bring us to faith in Christ so that we can be saved. If the doctrine of total depravity, as we have unfolded it in the previous chapter, is true, there can be no salvation without the reality of irresistible grace. If we are dead in our sins, and unable to submit to God because of our rebellious nature, then we will never believe in Christ unless God overcomes our rebellion.

Someone may say, "Yes, the Holy Spirit must draw us to God, but we can use our freedom to resist or accept that drawing." But that is not what the Bible teaches. Except for the continual exertion of saving grace, we will always use our freedom to resist God. That is what it means to be "unable to submit to God." "The mind that is set on the flesh is hostile to God, for it does not submit to God's law; indeed, it *cannot*. Those who are in the flesh *cannot* please God" (Rom. 8:7-8).

If a person becomes humble enough to submit to God, it is because God has given that person a new, humble nature. If a person remains too hard-hearted and proud to submit to God, it is because that person has not been given such a willing spirit. But to see this most persuasively, we should look at the Scriptures.

Unless the Father Draws

In John 6:44, Jesus says, "No one can come to me unless the Father who sent me draws him." This drawing is the sovereign work of grace without which none of us will be saved from our rebellion against God. Again some may object, "He draws *all* men, not just some." Then they may cite John 12:32, "And I,

27

when I am lifted up from the earth, will *draw all people* to myself."

But there are several serious problems with this objection. One is that the word translated "all people" is simply "all" (Greek *pantas*). There is no word for "people." Jesus simply says: "When I am lifted up, I will draw *all* to myself." When we see that we have to ask from similar contexts in John what this "all" probably refers to.

One similar context is in the previous chapter—John 11:50-52. Caiaphas the high priest is speaking more truly than he knows, John says.

> " ... Nor do you understand that it is better for you that one man should die for the people, not that the whole nation should perish." He did not say this of his own accord, but being high priest that year he prophesied that Jesus would die for the nation, and not for the nation only, but also to gather into one the children of God who are scattered abroad.

These last words describe the scope of Jesus's death as John presents it in this Gospel. Jesus died not just for one ethnic group, but "to gather into one the children of God who are scattered abroad"—*all* of them. This is a reference to Gentiles whom God will effectively draw to himself when they hear the gospel. They are called "children of God" because God has chosen them to be adopted, as Paul says in Ephesians 1:4-5.

So if this is a good parallel, then the *all* in John 12:32 is not all human beings, but "all the children of God." "When I am lifted up from the earth, I will draw all the *children of God* to myself." From every tribe and tongue and people and nation (Rev. 5:9).

Or you could say, "I will draw *all* of my sheep," because Jesus says in John 10:15, "I lay down my life for the sheep"—*all* of them. And in John 10:27, "My sheep hear my voice, and I know them, and they follow me"—*all* of them. Or you could say, "I will draw *all* who are of the truth," because Jesus says in John 18:37, "*Everyone* who is of the truth listens to my voice." Or you could say, "I will draw all who are of God," because Jesus says in John 8:47, "*Whoever* is of God hears the words of God." Or you could say, "I will draw *all* that the Father gives to me," because John 6:37 says, "*All* that the Father gives me will come to me."

In other words, running straight through the Gospel of John is the truth that God the Father and God the Son decisively draw people out of darkness into light. And Christ died for this. He was lifted up for this—that *all* of them might be drawn to him—*all* the children, *all* the sheep, *all* who are of the truth, *all* those whom the Father gives to the Son. What John 12:32 adds is that this happens today in history by pointing the whole world to the crucified Christ and preaching the good news that whoever believes on him will be saved. In that preaching of the lifted up Christ, God opens the ears of the deaf. The sheep hear his voice and follow Jesus (John 10:16, 27).

But the main objection to using John 12:32 (draw all) to deny that the drawing of John 6:44 ("No one can come to me unless the Father who sent me draws him") actually produces the coming, is the way John describes the relationship between God's drawing and the failure of Judas to follow Jesus to the end.

In John 6:64-65 Jesus says,

> "There are some of you who do not believe." (For Jesus knew from the beginning who those were who did not believe, and who it was who would betray him.) And he said, "This is why I told you that no one can come to me unless it is granted him by the Father."

Notice that Jesus says the reason he said (back in John 6:44) that "no one can come to me unless it is granted him (=is drawn) by the Father," is to explain why "there are some of you who do not believe." We could paraphrase it like this: Jesus knew from the beginning that Judas would not believe on him in spite of all the teaching and invitations he received. And because he knew this, he explains it with the words, "No one comes to me unless it is given to him by my Father."

There were many influences in the life of Judas for good—in that sense Judas was wooed, and entreated, and drawn for three years. But the point of Jesus in John 6:44 and 6:65 is that Judas's resistance to grace was not the ultimately decisive factor. What was ultimately decisive was that it was not "granted him" to come. He was not "drawn" by the Father. The decisive, *irresistible* gift of grace was not given. This is why we speak of "irresistible grace." In ourselves we are all just as resistant to grace as Judas. And the reason any of us has come to Jesus is not that we are smarter, or wiser, or more virtuous than Judas, but that the Father overcame our resistance and drew us to Christ. All are saved by irresistible grace—amazing grace!

> Long my imprisoned spirit lay,
>
> Fast bound in sin and nature's night;
>
> Thine eye diffused a quickening ray—
>
> I woke, the dungeon flamed with light;
>
> My chains fell off, my heart was free,
>
> I rose, went forth, and followed Thee.

This is what happens when the Father "draws us" irresistibly and infallibly to Jesus.

The Requirements for Salvation As Gifts of God

Now consider the way Paul describes repentance as a gift of God. In 2 Timothy 2:24-25 he says, "The Lord's servant must not be quarrelsome but kind to everyone, able to teach, patiently enduring evil, correcting his opponents with gentleness. *God may perhaps grant them repentance* leading to a knowledge of the truth."

Just as Jesus in John 6:65 said that coming to Jesus was "granted" by the Father, so here Paul says that repentance is "granted" by God. "God may perhaps grant them repentance." Notice, he is not saying merely that salvation is a gift of God. He is saying that the requirements for salvation are also a gift. When a person hears a preacher say, "Repent, and come to Christ," he can choose to resist that call. He can disobey. He can say, "No, I will not repent."

But if God *gives* him repentance, he cannot resist because the very meaning of the gift of repentance is that God has changed our heart and made it willing to repent. In other words the gift of repentance is the overcoming of resistance to repentance. This is why we call this work of God "*irresistible* grace." Resistance to repentance is replaced by the gift of repentance. That is how all of us came to repent.

Thousands of truly repentant people do not know this. They have been taught erroneous things about how they were converted, and therefore they are stunted in their worship and love. Perhaps you have been one of them. If that is true, don't be angry at your teachers, rejoice with great joy that you have seen 2 Timothy 2:25, and let your heart overflow with thankfulness and brokenhearted joy at the new awareness at how amazing your repentance is. It is an absolutely free gift of God's grace. Which means he loves you more particularly than you have ever thought.

Never Against Our Will

It should be obvious from this that irresistible grace never implies that God forces us to repent or believe or follow Jesus against our will. That would even be a contradiction in terms because believing and repenting and following are always willing, or they are hypocrisy. Irresistible grace does not drag the unwilling into the kingdom, it makes the unwilling willing. It does not work with constraint from the outside, like hooks and chains; it works with power from the inside, like new thirst and hunger and compelling desire.

Therefore irresistible grace is compatible with preaching and witnessing that tries to persuade people to do what is reasonable and what will accord with their best interests. God uses the ministry of the word to accomplish his supernatural changes in the heart. These changes bring about repentance and faith.

Paul writes in 1 Corinthians 1:23-24, "We preach Christ crucified, a stumbling block to Jews and folly to Gentiles, but to those who are called, both Jews and Greeks, Christ the power of God and the wisdom of God." Notice the two kinds of "calls" implied in this text.

First, the preaching of Paul goes out to all, both Jews and Greeks. This is a *general* call of the gospel. It offers salvation impartially and indiscriminately to all. Whoever will believe on the crucified Christ will have him as Savior and Lord. But often this general call to everyone falls on unreceptive ears and is called foolishness.

But notice, secondly, that Paul refers to another kind of *call*. He says that among those who hear, both Jews and Greeks, there are some who, in addition to hearing the general call, are "called" in another way. "But to those who are called, both Jews and Greeks, Christ the power of God and the wisdom of God" (v. 24). In other words they are called in such a way that they no longer regard the cross as foolishness but as the wisdom and power of God.

Something happened in their hearts that changed the way they saw Christ. Let's describe this not as the general call but as the effectual call of God. This is like the call of Lazarus out of the grave. Jesus called with a loud voice, "Lazarus, come out" (John 11:43). And the dead man came out. This kind of call creates what it calls for. If it says, "Live!" it creates life. If it says, "Repent!" it creates repentance. If it says "Believe!" it creates faith. If it says "Follow me!" it creates obedience. Paul says that everyone who is called in this sense no longer regards the cross as foolishness, but regards the cross as the power of God. They are not coming to Christ under coercion. They are acting freely from what they truly value as infinitely precious. That is what has happened to them. Their resistance to the cross has been overcome because the call of God broke through their spiritual blindness and granted them to see it as wisdom and power. This is what we mean by irresistible grace.

At Work Beneath Our Will

How God works to change our will without coercion against our will is further explained in 2 Corinthians 4:4-6:

> The god of this world has blinded the minds of the unbelievers, to keep them from seeing the light of the gospel of the glory of Christ, who is the image of God. For what we proclaim is not ourselves, but Jesus Christ as Lord, with ourselves as your servants for Jesus' sake. For God, who said, "Let light shine out of darkness," has shone in our hearts to give the light of the knowledge of the glory of God in the face of Jesus Christ.

Since men are blind to the worth of Christ, a miracle is needed in order for them to come to see and believe. Paul compares this miracle with the first day of creation when God said, "Let there be light." One of the most wonderful statements about how all of us were brought from blindness to sight—from bondage to freedom, from death to life—is: "God has shone in our hearts to give the light of the knowledge of the glory of God in the face of Jesus Christ." A real light—a spiritual light—shone in our hearts. It was the "light of the knowledge of the glory of God in the face of Christ" (v. 6). Or as verse 4 puts it, "the light of the gospel of the glory of Christ, who is the image of God." In other words, God causes the glory—the self-authenticating truth and beauty—of Christ to be seen and savored in our hearts.

From that moment on our will toward Christ is fundamentally altered. This is in fact a new creation—a new birth. This is essentially the same divine act as the effectual call that we saw in 1 Corinthians 1:24, "To those who are called ... Christ [has now been seen as] the power of God and the wisdom of God." Those who are called have their eyes opened by the sovereign, creative power of God so that they no longer see the cross as foolishness but as the power and the wisdom of God. The effectual call is the miracle of having our blindness removed. God causes the glory of Christ to shine with irresistible beauty. This is irresistible grace.

"The Lord Opened Her Heart"

Another example of it is in Acts 16:14, where Lydia is listening to the preaching of Paul. Luke says, "The Lord opened her heart to pay attention to what was said by Paul." Unless God opens our hearts, we will not hear the truth and beauty of Christ in the message of the gospel. This heart-opening is what we mean by irresistible grace. It overcomes the willful resistance of blindness to beauty and deafness to the goodness of the good news.

Another way to describe it is "new birth" or being born again. New birth is a miraculous creation of God that enables a formerly "dead" person to receive Christ and so be saved. We do not bring about the new birth by our faith. God brings about our faith by the new birth. Notice the way John expresses this relationship in 1 John 5:1: "Everyone who believes that Jesus is the Christ has been born of God." This means that being born of God comes first and believing follows. Believing in Jesus is not the cause of being born again; it is the evidence that we "have been born of God."

New Birth: An Act of Sovereign Creation

To confirm this, notice from John's Gospel how our receiving Christ relates to being born of God. "To all who did receive him, who believed in his name, he gave the right to become children of God, who were born, not of blood nor of the will of the flesh nor of the will of man, but of God" (John 1:12-13). So John says that God gives the right to become the children of God to all who receive Christ (v. 12). Then he goes on to say that those who do receive Christ "were born, not of blood nor of the will of the flesh nor of the will of man, but of God." In other words, it is necessary to receive Christ in order to become a child of God, but the birth that brings one into the family of God is not possible by the will of man. Only God can do it.

Man is dead in trespasses and sins (Eph. 2:1). He cannot make himself new, or create new life in himself. He must be born of God. Then, with the new nature of God, he sees Christ for who he really is, and freely receives Christ for all that he is. The two acts (new birth and faith) are so closely connected that in experience we cannot distinguish them. God begets us anew and the first glimmer of life in the newborn child is faith. Thus new birth is the effect of irresistible grace, because it is an act of sovereign creation—"not of the will of man but of God." This glorious truth of the new birth and how it happens is so wonderful that I wrote a whole book about it called, *Finally Alive: What Happens When We Are Born Again*. If you want to go deeper into the wonders of irresistible grace, that might be a good place to turn.

We began this chapter by saying that most Christians know intuitively that God's grace has been decisive in bringing about our conversion. We look at those who resist the gospel and say with trembling, "But for the grace of God, there go I." Now at the end of the chapter I hope it is clearer why that is. God really did overcome out resistance. He really did draw us to himself. He really did grant us repentance. He really did cause us to be born again so that we received Christ. He really did shine in our hearts to give the light of the glory of Christ. He really did call us—like Lazarus—from death to life. It is not surprising then, that all true Christians, even before we have been taught these things, know intuitively that grace was decisive in bringing us to Christ.

Often the heart precedes the head into the truth. That is surely the case for many Christians in regard to irresistible grace. But now we have seen this truth for ourselves in God's word. My prayer is that because of this you will go even deeper in your experience of the grace of God. May you worship God and love people as never before. That is what a profound experience of sovereign grace does.

5
LIMITED ATONEMENT

The Atonement is the work of God in Christ on the cross in which he completed the work of his perfectly righteous life, canceled the debt of our sin, appeased his holy wrath against us, and won for us all the benefits of salvation. The death of Christ was necessary because God would not show a just regard for his glory if he swept sins under the rug with no recompense. That's the point of Romans 3:25-26:

> God put [Christ] forward as a propitiation by his blood, to be received by faith. This was *to show God's righteousness*, because in his divine forbearance he had passed over former sins. It was *to show his righteousness at the present time, so that he might be just* and the justifier of the one who has faith in Jesus.

You can see from the emphasized words that the death of Christ was necessary to vindicate the righteousness of God in justifying the ungodly by faith. Why is that? Because it would be unrighteous to acquit sinners as though their sin was insignificant, when in fact sin is an insult against the value of God's glory. And since the value of God's glory is infinite, the offense is infinitely outrageous. Therefore Jesus bears the curse, which was due to our sin, so that we can be justified and the righteousness of God can be vindicated.

What Did Christ Actually Achieve?

The term "limited atonement" addresses the question, "For whom did Christ do all this?" "For whom did he die?" "Whose sin did he atone for?" "For whom did he purchase all the benefits of salvation?" But behind these questions of the *extent* of the atonement lies the equally important question about the *nature* of the atonement. What did Christ actually achieve on the cross for those for whom he died? That question will lead to a more accurate answer to the others.

If you say that he died for every human being *in the same way*, then you have to define the *nature* of the atonement very differently than you would if you believed that Christ, *in some particular way*, died for those who actually do believe. In the first case, you would believe that the death of Christ did not *decisively secure* the salvation of anyone; it only made all men savable so that something else would be decisive in saving them, namely their choice. In that case, the death of Christ did not actually remove the sentence of death and did not actually guarantee new life for anyone. Rather it only created possibilities of salvation which could be actualized by people who provide the decisive cause, namely their faith. In this understanding of the atonement, faith and repentance are not blood-bought gifts of God for particular sinners, but are rather the acts of some sinners that make the blood work for them.

You begin to see how closely this doctrine of the atonement is connected with the previous one, irresistible grace. What I think the Bible teaches is that this very irresistible grace is purchased by the blood of Jesus. The new birth is blood-bought. The effectual call is blood-bought. The gift of repentance is blood-bought. None of these acts of irresistible grace is deserved. They came to us because Christ secured them by his blood and righteousness. But that means, he did not secure them for all in the same way. Otherwise all would be born again, and all would be effectually called, and all would receive the gift of repentance.

So the personal and experiential question we face here at the beginning of this chapter is: Do we believe that Christ decisively secured for me the call and life and faith and repentance I now have? Or do I contribute these things from myself so that what he died to achieve counts for me? For if Christ died for all people in the same way, then his death did not infallibly obtain regenerating grace or faith or repentance for those who are saved. We must have regenerated ourselves without the blood-bought miracle of Christ, and we must have come to faith and repentance ourselves without the blood-bought gifts of faith and repentance.

In other words, if we believe that Christ died for all men in the same way, then the benefits of the cross cannot include the mercy by which we are brought to faith, because then all men would be brought to faith, but they aren't. But if the mercy by which we are brought to faith (irresistible grace) is not part of what Christ purchased on the cross, then we are left to obtain our deliverance from deadness and blindness and rebellion another way. We are left to make our way into the safety of Christ another way, since he did not obtain this entrance (new birth, faith, repentance) for us when he died.

Who Really Limits the Atonement

Therefore, it becomes evident that it is not the Calvinist who limits the atonement. It is those who deny that the atoning death of Christ accomplishes what we most desperately need—

namely, salvation from the condition of deadness and hardness and blindness under the wrath of God. They limit the power and effectiveness of the atonement so that they can say that it was accomplished even for those who die in unbelief and are condemned. In order to say that Christ died for all men in the same way, they must limit the atonement to a *possibility* or an *opportunity* for salvation if fallen humans can escape from their deadness and rebellion and obtain faith by an effectual means not provided by the cross.

On the other hand, we do not limit the power and effectiveness of the atonement. Rather we say that in the cross, God had in view the actual, effective redemption of his children from all that would destroy them, including their own unbelief. And we affirm that when Christ died particularly for his bride, he did not simply create a possibility or an opportunity for salvation, but really purchased and infallibly secured for them all that is necessary to get them saved, including the grace of regeneration and the gift of faith.

We do not deny that Christ died to save all *in some sense*. Paul says in 1 Timothy 4:10 that in Christ God is "the Savior of all people, especially of those who believe." What we deny is that the death of Christ is for all men in the *same* sense. God sent Christ to save *all* in some sense. And he sent Christ to save those who believe in *a more particular sense*. God's intention is different for each. That is a natural way to read 1 Timothy 4:10.

For "all men" the death of Christ is the foundation of the free offer of the gospel. This is the meaning of John 3:16, "God so loved the world, that he gave his only Son, that whoever believes in him should not perish but have eternal life." The sending of the Son is for the whole world in the sense that Jesus makes plain: *so that whoever believes in him should not perish*. In that sense God sent Jesus for everyone. Or, to use the words of 1 Timothy 4:10, God is the "Savior of all people" in that Christ died to provide an absolutely reliable and valid offer of forgiveness to all, such that everyone, without exception, who trusts Christ would be saved.

When the gospel is preached, Christ is offered to all without discrimination. And the offer is absolutely authentic for all. What is offered is Christ, and anyone—absolutely anyone—who receives Christ receives all that he bought for his sheep, his bride. The gospel does not *offer* a possibility of salvation. It *is* the possibility of salvation. But what is offered is Christ, and in him the infinite achievement that he accomplished for his people by his death and resurrection.

The Crucial Role of the New Covenant[1]

The biblical foundation for saying that Christ died not just to make salvation available for all who believe, but to actually purchase the faith of the elect is the fact that the blood of Jesus secured the blessings of the new covenant for his people. The faith of God's chosen and called was purchased by "the blood of the covenant" (Matt. 26:28).

The Arminian view portrays sinners as needing divine assistance in order to believe. That's true. We do need assistance. But more assistance than Arminianism assumes. In that view the sinner, after being assisted by God, provides the decisive impulse. God only assists; the sinner decides. Thus, "the blood of the covenant" does not decisively secure our faith. The decisive cause of faith is human self-determination. The atoning work of Christ, they say, sets up this possibility. But it does not

---

1   The argument that follows is developed more fully in John Piper, "'My Glory I Will Not Give to Another': Preaching the Fullness of Definite Atonement for the Glory of God," in David and Jonathan Gibson, eds, *From Heaven He Came and Sought Her: Definite Atonement in Historical, Biblical, Theological, and Pastoral Perspective* (Wheaton, Illinois: Crossway, 2013).

secure the outcome. But the new covenant, bought by the blood of Christ, teaches something very different. Let's put the teaching of the new covenant before us.

God spoke the terms of the new covenant through Jeremiah:

> The days are coming, declares the LORD, when I will make a *new covenant* with the house of Israel and the house of Judah, not like the covenant that I made with their fathers ... my covenant that they broke, though I was their husband, declares the LORD. For this is the covenant that I will make with the house of Israel after those days, declares the LORD: I will put my law within them, and I will write it on their hearts. And ... I will forgive their iniquity, and I will remember their sin no more. (Jer. 31:31-34)

One fundamental difference between the promised new covenant and the old one "made with their fathers" is that they broke the old one, but in the new covenant, God will "put the law within them" and will "write it on their hearts" so that the conditions of the covenant are secured by God's sovereign initiative. The new covenant will not be broken. That is part of its design. It lays claim on its participants, secures them, and keeps them.

God makes this point even more clearly in the next chapter of Jeremiah:

> I will give them one heart and one way, that they may fear me forever, for their own good and the good of their children after them. I will make with them an everlasting covenant, that I will not turn away from doing good to them. And I will put the fear of me in their hearts, that they may not turn from me. I will rejoice in doing them good. (Jer. 32:39-41)

God makes at least six promises in this text: 1) I will make with them an everlasting covenant; 2) I will give them the kind of heart that secures their fearing me forever; 3) I will never turn away from doing good to them; 4) I will put the fear of me in their hearts; 5) I will not let them turn away from me; and 6) I will rejoice in doing good to them.

Here in Jeremiah 32 it becomes even clearer than in Jeremiah 31 that God is taking the sovereign initiative to make sure that the covenant succeeds. God will not leave it finally in the power of the fallen human will to attain or sustain membership in the new covenant. He will give a new heart—a heart that fears the Lord. It will be decisively God's doing, not man's. And he will act in this covenant so that "they may not turn from me" (Jer. 32:40). Thus John Owen comments, "This then is one main difference of these two covenants—that the Lord did in the old only require the condition; now, in the new, he will also effect it in all the federates, to whom this covenant is extended."[2]

Similarly, Ezekiel prophesies in the same way: God will take the initiative and give a new heart and a new spirit.

> I will give them one heart, and a new spirit I will put within them. I will remove the heart of stone from their flesh and give them a heart of flesh. (Ezek. 11:19)

> I will give you a new heart, and a new spirit I will put within you. And I will remove the heart of stone from your flesh and give you a heart of flesh. And I will put my Spirit within you, and cause you to walk in my statutes and be careful to obey my rules. (Ezek. 36:26-27)

An unregenerate heart of stone is the deep reason why Israel did not trust God's promises, or love him with all their heart and

---

2   John Owen, *The Death of Death in the Death of Christ,* in *The Works of John Owen,* ed. W. H. Goold, 16 vols. (Edinburgh: The Banner of Truth Trust, 1967 [1850-1853]), 10:237.

soul and mind and strength. If the new covenant is to be more successful than the old covenant, God will have to take out the heart of stone and give his people a heart that loves him. In other words, he will have to take a miraculous initiative to secure the faith and love of his people. This is exactly what Moses says God will do:

> The LORD your God will circumcise your heart and the heart of your offspring, so that you will love the LORD your God with all your heart and with all your soul, that you may live. (Deut. 30:6)

In other words, in the new covenant God promises that he will take the initiative and will create a new heart, so that people are made members of the new covenant by his initiative, not their own. If someone enjoys participation in the new covenant with all its blessings, it is because God forgave his iniquity, removed his heart of stone, gave him a tender heart of flesh that fears and loves God, and caused him to walk in his statutes. In other words, the new covenant promises regeneration. It promises to create faith and love and obedience where before there was only hardness.

The Blood of Jesus Obtains the Promises of the New Covenant
What we find when we come to the New Testament is that Jesus is the Mediator of this new covenant and that he secured it by his own blood. This is the connection between the atonement and the new covenant: Jesus' blood is the blood of the covenant. The design of his death was to establish this covenant with all the terms we have just seen.

According to Luke 22:20, at the Last Supper, Jesus took the cup after they had eaten and said, "This cup that is poured out for you is the new covenant in my blood." Paul recounts this in 1 Corinthians 11:25: "He took the cup, after supper, saying, 'This cup is the new covenant in my blood.'" I take this to mean that the promises of the new covenant are purchased by the blood of Christ. Or to use the language of Hebrews, "This makes Jesus the guarantor of a better covenant" (Heb. 7:22). "He is the mediator of a new covenant, so that those who are called may receive the promised eternal inheritance" (Heb. 9:15).

Therefore all the promises of the new covenant are blood-bought promises. When they come true for us they come true because Jesus died to make them come true. This means that the particular promises of the new covenant to create a people of God and keep a people of God are what Jesus died for.

The point I am making is that not all the promises of the new covenant depend on the condition of faith. Rather, one of the promises made in the new covenant is that the condition of faith *itself* will be given by God. That's why I say that the new covenant people are created and preserved by God. "I will put the fear of me in their hearts, that they may not turn from me" (Jer. 32:40). God puts the fear of God in us in the first place. And God keeps us from turning away. He creates his new people and keeps his new people. And he does this by the blood of the covenant, which Jesus said was his own blood (Luke 22:20).

The upshot of this understanding of the new covenant is that there is a definite atonement for the new covenant people. In the death of Christ, God secures a definite group of unworthy sinners as his own people by purchasing and guaranteeing the conditions they must meet to be part of his people. The blood of the covenant—Christ's blood—purchases and guarantees the new heart of faith and repentance. God did not do this for everyone. He did it for a "definite" or a "particular" group, owing to nothing in themselves. And since he did it through Jesus Christ, the Great Shepherd, who laid down his life for the sheep, we say, "to [him] be glory forever and ever" (Heb. 13:21). This achievement is a great part of the glory of the cross of Christ.

Jesus Lays Down His Life for the Sheep

There are many Scriptures which support what we have just seen, and teach that God's purpose in the death of Christ included the ingathering of a new-covenant people by means of his irresistible grace.

For example, in John 10:15 Jesus says, "I lay down my life for the sheep." This is not the same as saying I lay down my life for all people. In John's Gospel "the sheep" are not everyone. Nor does the term "sheep" refer to those who have used their power of self-determination to produce faith. Rather they are those whom God has chosen and given to the Son (John 6:37, 44). Their faith is possible because they are sheep.

We see this in John 10:26 where Jesus says, "You do not believe, because you do not belong to my sheep." In other words, being a sheep enables you to believe, not vice versa. So the sheep do not first make themselves sheep by believing; they are able to believe because they are sheep. So when Jesus says, "I lay down my life for the sheep," he means, by my blood I purchase those my Father has given to me, and I secure their faith and all the blessings that come to those who are united with me.

John 17 points in the same direction. Jesus limits his prayer in John 17 to his sheep—those whom the Father has given him.

> I have manifested your name to the people whom you gave me out of the world. Yours they were, and you gave them to me ... I am praying for them. I am not praying for the world but for those whom you have given me, for they are yours... And for their sake I consecrate myself, that they also may be sanctified in truth. (John 17:6, 9, 19)

The consecration in view here is the death of Jesus which he is about to undergo. Therefore he is saying that his death is designed especially for those for whom he is praying. "I am not praying for the world but for those whom you have given me" (John 17:9). And for these he is consecrating himself. For these he is laying down his life.

Jesus Died to Gather the Children of God

John tells us of a prophecy coming from the high priest which makes a similar point.

> "Nor do you understand that it is better for you that one man should die for the people, not that the whole nation should perish." He did not say this of his own accord, but being high priest that year he prophesied that Jesus would die for the nation, and not for the nation only, but also to gather into one the children of God who are scattered abroad. (John 11:50-52)

There are "children of God" scattered throughout the world. These are the "sheep"—the ones the Father has given to the Son and will irresistibly draw to Jesus. Jesus died to gather these people into one flock. The point is the same as John 10:15-16: "I lay down my life for the sheep. And I have other sheep that are not of this fold; *I must bring them also*, and they will listen to my voice." The "gathering" in John 11:52 and the "bringing" in John 10:16 are the same work of God. And both are the divine design of the cross of Christ. Christ did not die just to make this possible, but to make this happen.

It is described again by John in Revelation 5:9 where heaven sings to Christ: "Worthy are you to take the scroll and to open its seals, for you were slain, and by your blood you ransomed people for God from every tribe and language and people and nation." In accordance with John 10:16, John does not say that the death of Christ ransomed all people but that it ransomed people *from* all the tribes of the world.

This is the way we may understand texts like 1 John 2:2, that some have used to argue against the doctrine of limited or definite atonement. In words very reminiscent of John 11:52 John says, "[Christ] is the propitiation for our sins, and not for ours only but also for the sins of the whole world." The question is: Does this mean that Christ died with the intention to appease the wrath of God for every person in the world? From all that we have seen so far from John's writing, it is not likely that it has that meaning. Rather the verbal parallel between John 11:51-52 and 1 John 2:2 is so close it is difficult to escape the conviction that the same thing is intended by John in both verses.

> "He prophesied that Jesus should die for the nation, and not for the nation only, but to gather into one the children of God who are scattered abroad." (John 11:51-2)

> "He is the propitiation for our sins, and not for ours only but also for the sins of the whole world." (1 John 2:2)

The "whole world" is parallel with "children of God scattered abroad." So it is natural to think that John's point in 1 John 2:2 is to stress that God's propitiating work in Christ is not parochial, as if he is only interested in Jews, or in one class or race. No grouping of humans should ever say, "He is the propitiation for our sins only." No. His propitiating work is meant to gather people from the "whole world." "I have other sheep that are not of this fold!" (John 10:16)—all over the world. These are the "sheep" for whom he died, the redeemed "children of God" scattered abroad, the ransomed people "from every tongue and tribe and people and nation."

A Ransom for Many

In harmony with what we have seen, for example, in Revelation 5:9 ("by your blood you ransomed people for God from every tribe"), Jesus said in Mark 10:45, "The Son of Man also came not to be served but to serve, and to give his life as a ransom for many." He does not say "ransom for all" but "ransom for many," just as Revelation 5:9 says "ransomed *from* every tribe." I know that the word "many" does not prove my case. "Many" could logically mean "all." My point is simply to show that "many" (rather than "all") fits with the limits we have seen already in this chapter.

Similarly in Matthew 26:28, Jesus says, at the last supper, "This is my blood of the covenant, which is poured out *for many* for the forgiveness of sins." And Hebrews 9:28 says, "So Christ, having been offered once to bear the *sins of many*, will appear a second time, not to deal with sin but to save those who are eagerly waiting for him." And Isaiah 53:12 says that the suffering servant "bore the sin *of many*."

Christ Gave Himself for the Church

One of the clearest passages on God's particular intention in the death of Christ is Ephesians 5:25-27.

> Husbands, love your wives, as Christ loved the church and gave himself up for her, that he might sanctify her, having cleansed her by the washing of water with the word, so that he might present the church to himself in splendor, without spot or wrinkle or any such thing, that she might be holy and without blemish.

Here Paul says that the intended beneficiary of the death of Christ is the church, the bride of Christ. One of the reasons I am jealous for this doctrine of limited atonement or particular redemption is that I want the bride of Christ to be properly moved by the particular love that Christ had for her when he died. This was not only a world-embracing love; it was a bride-purchasing love. God knew those who were his. And he sent his Son to obtain this bride for this Son.

> From heaven he came and sought her
>
> To be his holy bride;
>
> With his own blood he bought her,
>
> And for her life he died.[3]

There is a particular love for the bride in this sacrifice that the church misses when she only thinks that God did not have any particular people in mind when he bought the church with his Son's blood. I used to say to the church I served, "I love all the women of this church, but I love my wife in a very special way." I would not want Noël to think that she is loved just because I love all women and she happens to be a woman. So it is with God and all the people of the world. There is a universal love for all, but there is a particular love that he has for the bride. And when Christ died, there was a particular aim in that death for her. He knew her from the foundation of the world, and he died to obtain her.

The Precious Logic of Romans 8:32

Another important text on this issue of the design and extent of the atonement is Romans 8:32. It is one of the most precious promises for God's people in all the Bible. Paul says, "He who did not spare his own Son but gave him up for us all, how will he not also with him graciously give us all things?" The unanswered question anticipates our ability to answer it and turn it into a rock solid promise: "Since God did not spare his own Son but gave him up for us all, he will most certainly give us all things with him." Who are the "us" in this verse? They are the people of verses 29-31:

---

3   Samuel J. Stone, "The Church's One Foundation", (http://www.hymnsite.com/lyrics/umh545.sht)

Those whom he foreknew he also predestined to be conformed to the image of his Son, in order that he might be the firstborn among *many brothers*. And *those* whom he predestined he also called, and *those* whom he called he also justified, and *those* whom he justified he also glorified. What then shall *we* say to these things? If God is for *us*, who can be against *us*?

The reason Paul can make such a staggering promise to "us" as he does in verse 32—that God will infallibly give us all things with him—is that the ones being addressed are the foreknown, the predestined, the called, the justified. These are the "sheep," the "children of God scattered abroad." And for these people, Paul says, the death of Christ is the unshakable, absolutely certain guarantee that they will receive all things with him. This is the wonderful logic of Romans 8:32.

But what becomes of this logic if God gave his Son in this way for thousands who do not receive all things, but in fact perish? The logic is destroyed. It becomes: "If God did not spare his own Son, but gave him up for all people in the world, then, since many of them are lost, it is not true that they will most certainly receive all things with him." That is not the point of the verse.

It says, Because of God's giving the Son for his people, those people—foreknown and predestined from the foundation of the world—will receive everything God has to give. Therefore, the design of God in giving the Son is not only a general offer to the whole world, but a rock solid securing of infinite riches for his people. My great desire is that God's people see this and go deeper into the grace of this particular redemption. We are loved specifically in the atonement, not just generally. Our future is secured particularly by the blood of Christ.

In summary, the biblical point of limited atonement is that in the death of Christ God had a particular design for his elect. He was purchasing not just a possibility for them to believe and be saved, but he was purchasing the belief itself. The conversion of God's elect is blood-bought. The overcoming of our deadness and rebellion against God is not performed decisively by us so that we then qualify for the atonement. God's sovereign grace overcomes our deadness and rebellion. And that grace is purchased for us in the death of Christ.

If we want to go deeper in our experience of God's grace this is an ocean of love for us to enjoy. God does not mean for the bride of his Son to only feel loved with general, world-embracing love. He means for her to feel ravished with the specificity of his affection that he set on her before the world existed. He means for us to feel a focused: "I chose you. And I sent my Son to die to have you."

This is what we offer the world. We don't hoard it for ourselves. And we don't abandon it by saying, all we have to offer the world is God's general love for all people. No, we offer this. We offer a full and complete and definite atonement. We offer Christ. We don't say, Come to a possibility. We say, Come to Christ. Receive Christ. And what we promise them if they come is that they will be united to him and his bride. And all that he bought for his bride will be theirs. All that he secured with absolute certainty will be their portion forever.

Their faith will prove them to be among the elect. And their coming to Christ will prove that they are already the particular beneficiaries of his particular redemption, his definite atonement.

To solidify this deepening of our experience of God's grace we turn now to the doctrine of election. For it is the elect for whom he died with this immeasurable design of everlasting love.

6
UNCONDITIONAL ELECTION

If all of us are so depraved that we cannot come to God without being born again by the irresistible grace of God, and if this particular grace is purchased by Christ on the cross, then it is clear that the salvation of any of us is owing to God's election. He chose those to whom he would show such irresistible grace, and for whom he would purchase it.

Election refers to God's choosing whom to save. It is unconditional in that there is no condition man must meet before God chooses to save him. Man is dead in trespasses and sins. So there is no condition he can meet before God chooses to save him from his deadness.

We are *not* saying that *final* salvation is unconditional. It is not. We must meet the condition of faith, for example, in Christ in order to inherit eternal life. But faith is not a condition for election. Just the reverse. Election is a condition for faith. It is because God chose us before the foundation of the world that he purchases our redemption at the cross, and then gives us spiritual life through irresistible grace, and brings us to faith.

Election Prior to Faith

Acts 13:48 reports how the Gentiles responded to the preaching of the gospel in Antioch of Pisidia. "And when the Gentiles heard this, they began rejoicing and glorifying the word of the Lord, and *as many as were appointed to eternal life believed.*" Notice, it does not say that as many as believed were chosen to be ordained to eternal life. It says that those who were ordained to eternal life (that is, those whom God had elected) believed. God's election preceded faith and made it possible. This is the decisive reason some believed while others did not.

Similarly Jesus says to the Jews in John 10:26, "You do not believe because you are not among my sheep." Notice again, he does not say, "You are not among my sheep because you do not believe." Who the sheep are is something God decides before we believe. It is the basis and enablement of our belief. "You do not believe, because you do not belong to my sheep." We believe because we are God's chosen sheep, not vice versa. (See also John 8:47; 18:37.)

Unconditionality in Romans 9[1]

In Romans 9, Paul stresses the unconditionality of election. In verses 11-12, he describes the principle God used in the choice of Jacob over Esau: "Though they were not yet born and had done nothing either good or bad, in order that God's purpose of election might continue, not because of works but because of his call, [Rebecca] was told, 'The elder will serve the younger.'" God's election is preserved in its unconditionality because it is transacted before we are born or have done any good or evil.

I know that some interpreters say that Romans 9 has nothing to do with the election of *individuals* to their *eternal* destinies, but only deals with corporate peoples in their historical roles. I think this is a mistake mainly because it simply does not come

---

1   Romans 9 is so foundational for the doctrine of unconditional election that I devoted an entire book to verses 1-23: John Piper, *The Justification of God: An Exegetical and Theological Study of Romans 9:1-23* (Grand Rapids: Baker Academic, 1993).

to terms with the problem Paul is addressing in the chapter. You can see this for yourself by reading the first five verses of Romans 9. When Paul says in Romans 9:6, "But it is not as though the word of God has failed," what is clear is that something has made it look as though God's promises have fallen. What is that?

The answer is given in verses 2 and 3. Paul says, "I have great sorrow and unceasing anguish in my heart. For I could wish that I myself were accursed and cut off from Christ for the sake of my brothers, my kinsmen according to the flesh." The deepest issue Paul is addressing is not why Israel as a nation has this or that historical role, but that individuals *within Israel* are accursed and *cut off from Christ*. In other words, *individual eternal* destinies are indeed at stake. And the nature of Paul's argument confirms this, because the first thing he says to confirm that the word of God has not failed is: "For not all who are descended from Israel belong to Israel" (Rom. 9:6). In other words, the individuals in Israel who perish were never part of the true Israel. Then he moves on to show how God's unconditional election was at work *within* Israel.[2]

The unconditionality of God's electing grace is stressed again in Romans 9:15-16: "'I will have mercy on whom I have mercy, and I will have compassion on whom I have compassion.' So then it depends not on human will or exertion, but on God, who has mercy." The very nature of the mercy we need is will-awakening, will-transforming mercy. We saw in the chapters on irresistible grace and total depravity that we are unable to love God or trust God or follow Christ. Our only hope is sovereign mercy, irresistible mercy. If that is true, what Paul says here makes sense. We are in no position to merit mercy or

---

2   More arguments for this understanding of Romans 9 are given in ibid, pp. 38-54.

elicit mercy. If we are to receive mercy it will be at God's free choice. That is what Paul says: "I will have mercy on whom I have mercy, and I will have compassion on whom I have compassion."

In Romans 11:7 Paul underlines again the individual nature of election within Israel: "Israel failed to obtain what it was seeking. The elect obtained it, but the rest were hardened." So throughout Romans 9–11 Paul assumes that election deals with individuals and with eternal destinies, and that it is unconditional. There is, I believe, a divine covenantal commitment to corporate Israel, but that does not contradict or annul the individual, eternal thrust of Romans 9. The principle of unconditionality is seen most clearly in Romans 9:11. God elects this way so that "though they were not yet born and had done nothing either good or bad, in order that God's purpose of election might continue."

Another Powerful Statement of Unconditionality
Ephesians 1:3-6 is another powerful statement of the unconditionality of our election and predestination to sonship.

> Blessed be the God and Father of our Lord Jesus Christ, who has blessed us in Christ with every spiritual blessing in the heavenly places, even as he chose us in him before the foundation of the world, that we should be holy and blameless before him. In love he predestined us for adoption as sons through Jesus Christ, according to the purpose of his will, to the praise of his glorious grace.

Some interpreters argue that this election before the foundation of the world was only an election of Christ, but not an election of which individuals would actually be in Christ. This simply amounts to saying that there is no unconditional election of individuals to salvation. Christ is put forward as the chosen one of God, and the salvation of individuals is dependent on their own initiative to overcome their depravity and be united to Christ by faith. God does not choose them, and therefore God cannot effectually convert them. He can only initiate conviction, but finally must wait to see who will provide the decisive impulse to quicken themselves from the dead and choose him.

This interpretation does not square well with verse 11 where it says that "we were predestined according to the purpose of him who *works all things according to the counsel of his will.*" Nor does it fit with the wording of verse 4. The ordinary meaning of the word for "choose" in verse 4 is to select or pick out of a group (see, for instance, Luke 6:13; 14:7; John 13:18; 15:16, 19). So the natural meaning of verse 4 is that God chooses his people from all humanity, before the foundation of the world by viewing them in relationship to Christ their redeemer. This is the natural way to read the verse.

It is true that all election is in relation to Christ. Christ was in the mind of God crucified before the foundation of the world (Rev. 13:8). There would be no election of sinners unto salvation if Christ were not appointed to die for their sins. So *in that sense* they are elect *in Christ*. But it is *they* who are chosen out of the world to be in Christ.

Also the wording of verse 5 suggests the election of people to be in Christ, and not just the election of Christ. Literally, it says, "Having predestined us unto sonship through Jesus Christ." *We* are the ones predestined, not Christ. He is the one that makes the election and predestination and adoption of sinners possible, and so our election is "through him," but there is no talk here about God having a view only to Christ in election. Christians come to faith and are united to Christ and covered by his blood because we were chosen before the foundation of the world for this destiny of holiness.

Perhaps the Most Important Text

Perhaps the most important text of all in relation to the teaching of unconditional election is Romans 8:28-33.

> We know that for those who love God all things work together for good, for those who are called according to his purpose. For those whom he foreknew he also predestined to be conformed to the image of his Son, in order that he might be the firstborn among many brothers. And those whom he predestined he also called, and those whom he called he also justified, and those whom he justified he also glorified. What then shall we say to these things? If God is for us, who can be against us? He who did not spare his own Son but gave him up for us all, how will he not also with him graciously give us all things? Who shall bring any charge against God's elect? It is God who justifies.

Often this text is used to argue against unconditional election on the basis of verse 29 which says that "those whom he *foreknew* he also predestined ...." So some say that people are not chosen unconditionally. They are chosen on the basis of their foreknown faith, which they produce without the help of irresistible grace and which God sees beforehand.

But this does not work with the way Paul develops his argument. Notice that Romans 8:30 says, "And those whom he predestined he also called, and those whom he called he also justified, and those whom he justified he also glorified." Focus for a moment on the fact that all whom God calls he also justifies.

This calling in verse 30 is not given to all people. The reason we know it's not is that *all* those who are called are also justified. There is an infallible connection between called and justified. "Those whom he called he also justified." But all people are not justified. Therefore all are not called. So this calling in verse 30 is not the general call to repentance that preachers give or that God gives through the glory of nature. Everybody receives that call. The call of verse 30 is given only to those whom God predestined to be conformed to the image of his Son (v. 29). And it is a call that leads necessarily to justification: "Those whom he called he also justified."

We know that justification only happens through faith. "We hold that one *is justified by faith* apart from works of the law" (Rom. 3:28; cf. 5:1). What then is this call that is given to all those who are predestined and which infallibly leads to justification? We have seen this before in chapter 4 when discussing irresistible grace. It is the call of 1 Corinthians 1:23-24, "We preach Christ crucified, a stumbling block to Jews and folly to Gentiles, but *to those who are called,* both Jews and Greeks, Christ the power of God and the wisdom of God." In other words, the calling is not the preaching, since that is done to all the Jews and Gentiles. Rather, the calling happens through the preaching in the hearts of some of the listeners. It wakens them from the dead and changes their perceptions of the cross so that they embrace it as God's wisdom and power. In other words, the *calling* of Romans 8:30 is irresistible, faith-creating grace.

Now consider the flow of Paul's thought again in Romans 8:30. "Those whom he predestined he also called, and those whom he called he also justified, and those whom he justified he also glorified." Between the act of predestination and justification, there is the act of calling. Since justification is only by faith, the calling in view must be the act of God whereby he calls faith into being. And since it always results in justification (all the called are justified), it must be sovereign. That is, it overcomes any resistance that gets in the way. So the calling of verse 30 is the sovereign work of God which brings a person to faith by which he is justified.

Now notice the implication this has for the meaning of foreknowledge in verse 29. When Paul says in verse 29, "Those whom he foreknew he also predestined," he can't mean (as so many try to make him mean) that God knows in advance who will use their free will to come to faith, so that he can predestine them to sonship because they made that free choice on their own. It can't mean that because we have just seen from verse 30 the decisive cause of faith in the justified is not the fallen human will but the sovereign call of God.

God does not foreknow those who come to faith apart from his creating the faith, because there are no such people. Whoever believes has been "called" into faith by the sovereign grace of God. When God looks from eternity into the future and sees the faith of the elect he sees his own work. And he chose to do that work for dead and blind and rebellious sinners unconditionally. For we were not capable of meeting the condition of faith. We were spiritually dead and blind.

So the foreknowledge of Romans 8:29 is not the mere awareness of something that will happen in the future apart from God's predetermination. Rather, it is the kind of knowledge referred to in Old Testament texts like Genesis 18:19 ("I have chosen [literally, *known*] him [Abraham] that he may command his children ... to keep the way of the Lord"), and Jeremiah 1:5 ("Before I formed you in the womb, I *knew* you, and before you were born I consecrated you; I appointed you a prophet to the nations"), and Amos 3:2 ("You [Israel] only have I *known* of all the families of the earth"). God "knows" all the families of the earth in one sense. But the meaning here is; You only, Israel, have I chosen for my own.

As C. E. B. Cranfield says, the foreknowledge of Romans 8:29 is "that special taking knowledge of a person which is God's electing grace." Such foreknowledge is virtually the same as election: "Those whom he foreknew (i.e., chose) he predestined to be conformed to the image of his Son."

Therefore, what this magnificent text (Rom. 8:28-33) teaches is that God really accomplishes the complete redemption of his people from start to finish. He foreknows (that is, elects) a people for himself before the foundation of the world, he predestines this people to be conformed to the image of his Son, he calls them to himself in faith, he justifies them through that faith alone, and he finally glorifies them. And nothing can separate them from the love of God in Christ forever and ever (Rom. 8:39). To him be all praise and glory!

If you are a believer in Christ, you have been loved by God from all eternity. He set his favor on you before the creation of the world. He chose you when he considered you in your helpless condition. He chose you for himself unconditionally. We may not boast in our election. That would be a profound misunderstanding of the meaning of unconditionality. When we had done nothing to commend ourselves to God in any way, he set his favor on us freely.

It was with us the way it was with the election of Israel: "It was not because you were more in number than any other people that the LORD set his love on you and chose you ... but it is because the LORD loves you" (Deut. 7:7-8). Read that carefully: he loves you because he loves you. He chose to do that in eternity. And because his love for you never had a beginning, it can have no end. What we are studying in this book is simply the way God works out that eternal love in history to save his own and bring us to the everlasting enjoyment of himself. May God take you deeper and deeper into the experience of this amazing sovereign grace.

7
PERSEVERANCE OF THE SAINTS

It follows from what we saw in the last chapter that the people of God *will* persevere to the end and not be lost. The foreknown are predestined, the predestined are called, the called are justified, and the justified are glorified (Rom. 8:30). No one is lost from this group. To belong to this people is to be eternally secure.

But we mean more than this by the doctrine of the perseverance of the saints. We mean that the saints will and must persevere *in faith and the obedience which comes from faith*. Election is unconditional, but glorification is not. There are many warnings in Scripture that those who do not hold fast to Christ can be lost in the end.

The following eight theses are my summary of this crucial doctrine.

1. Our faith must endure to the end if we are to be saved.
This means that the gospel is God's instrument in the preservation of faith as well as the begetting of faith. We do not act with a kind of cavalier indifference to the call for perseverance just because a person has professed faith in Christ, as though we can be assured from our perspective that they are now beyond the reach of the evil one. There is a fight of faith to be fought. The

elect will fight that fight. And by God's sovereign grace they will win it. We must endure to the end in faith if we are to be saved.

In 1 Corinthians 15:1-2 Paul shows the necessity of perseverance: "Now I would remind you, brothers, of the gospel I preached to you, which you received, in which you stand, and by which you are being saved, *if you hold fast to the word I preached to you—unless you believed in vain.*" This "if you hold fast" shows that there is a false start in the Christian life. Jesus told the parable of the soils to warn against these kinds of false beginnings:

> As for what was sown on rocky ground, this is the one who hears the word and immediately receives it with joy, yet he has no root in himself, but endures for a while, and when tribulation or persecution arises on account of the word, immediately he falls away. As for what was sown among thorns, this is the one who hears the word, but the cares of the world and the deceitfulness of riches choke the word, and it proves unfruitful. (Matt. 13:20-22)

In other words, there is, as Paul says in 1 Corinthians 15:2, a "believing in vain"—which means a false believing, a coming to Christ for reasons that don't include a love for his glory and hatred for our sin. The evidence, Paul says, that our faith is genuine is that we "hold fast to the word"—that we persevere.

Similarly Paul says in Colossians 1:21-23: "And you, who once were alienated and hostile in mind, doing evil deeds, he has now reconciled in his body of flesh by his death, in order to present you holy and blameless and above reproach before him, *if indeed you continue in the faith*, stable and steadfast, not shifting from the hope of the gospel." And again in 2 Timothy 2:11-12: "The saying is trustworthy, for: If we have died with him, we will also live with him; *if we endure, we will also reign with him.*"

Paul is following the teaching of Jesus in these words. Jesus said in Mark 13:13, "*The one who endures to the end* will be saved." And after his resurrection Jesus said to the churches in Revelation, "To the one who conquers I will grant to eat of the tree of life" (Rev. 2:7). "Be faithful unto death, and I will give you the crown of life" (Rev. 2:10; cf. 2:17, 25-26; 3:5, 11-12, 21). This is what we mean by the necessity of perseverance—the statement that we *must* persevere.

But a clarification is in order. Persevering in faith does not mean that the saints do not go through seasons of doubt and spiritual darkness and measures of unbelief in the promises and the goodness of God. "I believe; help my unbelief!" (Mark 9:24) is not a contradictory prayer. Measures of unbelief can coexist with a true faith.

Therefore what we mean when we say that faith must persevere to the end is that we must never come to a point of renouncing Christ with such hardness of heart that we can never return, but instead only prove ourselves to have been hypocrites in our professed faith. An example of such hardness is Esau.

> See to it that no one fails to obtain the grace of God; ... that no one is sexually immoral or unholy like Esau, who sold his birthright for a single meal. For you know that afterward, when he desired to inherit the blessing, he was rejected, for he found no chance to repent, though he sought it [repentance] with tears. (Heb. 12:15-17)

Esau became so spiritually hard and calloused in his love for this world that when he tried to repent he couldn't. All he could do is weep over the consequences of his folly, not the true ugliness of his sin or the dishonor he had heaped upon God in preferring a single meal to his entire God-given, God-accompanying birthright.

On the other hand the New Testament is at pains to make sure we do not despair thinking that backsliding and waywardness in sin is a one-way street. It is possible to repent and return. That process of wandering and returning is included in "the perseverance of the saints." For example, James says, "Whoever brings back a sinner from his wandering will save his soul from death and will cover a multitude of sins" (James 5:20). And John says, "If anyone sees his brother committing a sin not leading to death, he shall ask, and God will give him life.... All wrongdoing is sin, but there is sin that does not lead to death" (1 John 5:16-17). John's aim here is clearly to give hope to those who might be tempted to despair, and to those who love them and pray for them. John began his letter the same way he is ending it: "If we say we have no sin, we deceive ourselves, and the truth is not in us. If we confess our sins, he is faithful and just to forgive us our sins and to cleanse us from all unrighteousness" (1 John 1:8-9).

So when we speak of the necessity (and certainty, see below) of perseverance we do not mean perfection. And we do not mean that there are no struggles or serious measures of unbelief. We must keep in mind all that we have seen so far in this book. Belonging to Christ is a supernatural reality brought about by God and preserved by God (Jer. 32:40). The saints are not marked most deeply by what they do but by who they are. They are born again. They are a new creation. They do not go in and out of this newness. It is God's work. And it is irrevocable. But the fruit of it in faith and obedience is a fight to the end. And perseverance says: The fight will be fought and will not be finally lost.

2. Obedience, evidencing inner renewal from God, is necessary for final salvation.

This is not to say that God demands perfection. It is clear from Philippians 3:12 that the New Testament does not hold out the demand that those who are justified in Christ Jesus by faith be sinlessly perfect in order to be finally saved. "Not that I have already obtained this or am already perfect, but I press on to make it my own, because Christ Jesus has made me his own" (see also 1 John 1:8-10, and Matt. 6:12). But the New Testament does demand that we be morally changed and walk in newness of life. For example:

- "Strive for peace with everyone, and for the holiness without which no one will see the Lord." (Heb. 12:14)

- "If you live according to the flesh you will die, but if by the Spirit you put to death the deeds of the body, you will live." (Rom. 8:13)

- "Now the works of the flesh are evident: immorality, impurity, sensuality, idolatry, sorcery, enmity, strife, jealousy, fits of anger, rivalries, dissensions, divisions, envy, drunkenness, orgies, and things like these. I warn you, as I warned you before, that those who do such things will not inherit the kingdom of God." (Gal. 5:19-21. See also Eph. 5:5 and 1 Cor. 6:10.)

- "And by this we know that we have come to know him, if we keep his commandments. Whoever says 'I know him' but does not keep his commandments is a liar, and the truth is not in him, but whoever keeps his word, in him truly the love of God is perfected. By this we may know that we are in him: whoever says he abides in him ought to walk in the same way in which he walked." (1 John 2:3-6. See also 1 John 3:4-10, 14; 4:20.)

- "So Jesus said to the Jews who had believed him, 'If you abide in my word, you are truly my disciples.'" (John 8:31. See also Luke 10:28; Matt. 6:14-15; 18:35; Gen. 18:19; 22:16-17; 26:4-5; 2 Tim. 2:19.)

Again let there be a caution lest anyone take these texts in a perfectionistic direction. John's First Epistle is written to help us maintain our biblical equilibrium here. On the one hand it says, "No one born of God makes a practice of sinning, for God's seed abides in him, and he cannot keep on sinning because he has been born of God" (1 John 3:9). But on the other hand it says, "If we say we have (not "had" but present tense, "have") no sin, we deceive ourselves, and the truth is not in us" (1 John 1:8). And: "I am writing these things to you so that you may not sin. But if anyone does sin, we have an advocate with the Father, Jesus Christ the righteous" (1 John 2:1).

The perseverance of the saints is not the guarantee of perfection, but rather that God will keep us fighting the fight of faith so that we hate our sin and never make any lasting peace with it.

3. God's elect cannot be lost.

This is why we believe in eternal security—namely, the eternal security of the elect. The implication is that God will so work in us that those whom he has chosen for eternal salvation will be enabled by him to persevere in faith to the end and fulfill, by the power of the Holy Spirit, the requirements for a new kind of life.

We have seen before the ironclad chain of divine work in Romans 8:30: "Those whom he predestined he also called; and those whom he called he also justified; and those whom he justified he also glorified." What is evident from this verse is that those who are effectually called into the hope of salvation will indeed persevere to the end and be glorified. There are no dropouts in this sequence. These are promises of God rooted in unconditional election in the first place and in the sovereign, converting, preserving grace that we have seen before. The links in this chain are unbreakable, because God's saving work is infallible and his new covenant commitments are irrevocable.

Again, Paul is following the teachings of his Lord Jesus:

> "My sheep hear my voice, and I know them, and they follow me. I give them eternal life, and they will never perish, and no one will snatch them out of my hand. My Father, who has given them to me, is greater than all, and no one is able to snatch them out of the Father's hand. I and the Father are one." (John 10:27-30; see also Eph. 1:4-5.)

We saw before that being a sheep of Jesus means being chosen by God and given to the Son. In other words, the promise of Jesus never to lose any of his sheep is the sovereign commitment of the Son of God to preserve the faith of the elect for whom he laid down his life.

4. There is a falling away of some believers, but if it persists, it shows that their faith was not genuine and they were not born of God.

1 John 2:19 says, "They went out from us, but they were not of us; for if they had been of us, they would have continued with us. But they went out, that it might become plain that they all are not of us." Similarly, the parable of the four soils as interpreted in Luke 8:9-14 pictures people who "hear the word, receive it with joy; but these have no root, they believe for a while and in time of testing fall away."

The fact that such a thing is possible is precisely why the ministry of the gospel in every local church must contain many admonitions to the church members to persevere in faith and not be entangled in those things which could possibly strangle them and result in their condemnation. Pastors do not know infallibly who of his listeners are the good soil and who are the bad. His warnings and exhortations to persevere are the way he helps the saints endure. They hear the warnings and take heed and thus authenticate their humble and good hearts of faith.

5. God justifies us completely through the first genuine act of saving faith, but this is the sort of faith that perseveres and bears fruit in the "obedience of faith".

The point here is the emphasis above on the necessity of persevering faith and obedience does not mean God is waiting to observe our perseverance and obedience before he declares us completely righteous in union with Jesus Christ. Romans 5:1 says that we "have been justified by faith." It is a past act. The first time we believe in Jesus we are united to Christ. In union with him, his righteousness is counted as ours, at that moment. Paul says that he aims to "be found in him, not having a righteousness of my own that comes from the law, but that which comes through faith in Christ, the righteousness from God that depends on faith" (Phil. 3:9).

The ground of our acceptance with God is Christ alone—his blood and righteousness. "For our sake he made him to be sin who knew no sin, so that in him we might become the righteousness of God" (2 Cor. 5:21). "By the one man's obedience the many will be made righteous" (Rom. 5:19). The role of our faith is not to be a performance of something virtuous that God rewards with salvation. The point is that faith is a receiving of Christ who performed what we could not, a punishment for our sin and provision of our perfection. Faith is not the ground of our acceptance but the means or the instrument of union with Christ who alone is the ground of our acceptance with God.

The role of the obedience in our justification is to give evidence that our faith is authentic. Deeds of love are not the ground of our first or final acceptance with God. Their function is to validate, and make public, the sovereign work of God giving us new birth and creating the new heart of faith. Paul puts it this way: "In Christ Jesus neither circumcision nor uncircumcision counts for anything, but only faith working through love" (Gal. 5:6). What counts with God in justification is the kind of faith that works through love. It is not our love that causes God to be 100 per cent for us. It is God being 100 per cent for us through faith in Christ that enables us to love. Love is a fruit of the Spirit. And we have received the Spirit by our first act of faith (Gal. 3:2).

Therefore, the necessity of perseverance in faith and obedience for final salvation does not mean he waits till the end before he accepts us, adopts us, and justifies us. We do not fight the fight of faith in order to make God be 100 per cent for us. That happened in our union with Christ on our first act of faith. Rather, fight because he is 100 per cent for us. Paul put it like this: "Not that I have already obtained this or am already perfect, but I press on to make it my own, *because Christ Jesus has made me his own*" (Phil. 3:12). Christ has made us his own. That is how we fight on. In the final judgment *according to* works (not on the basis of works), the point of those works in the divine courtroom in relation to justification will be as public evidence of unseen faith and union with Christ. Christ will be the sole ground of our acceptance then as now.

6. God works to cause his elect to persevere.

We are not left to ourselves in the fight of faith, and our assurance is rooted in the sovereign love of God to perform what he has called us to do. The texts that follow here are all expressions of the new covenant that we discussed in chapter 5. Jesus purchased for us all the promises of God when he shed his blood (Luke 22:20; 2 Cor. 1:20).

One of the most precious of all those promises relates the new covenant to God's absolute commitment to cause us to persevere: "I will make with them an everlasting covenant, that I will not turn away from doing good to them. And *I will put the fear of me in their hearts, that they may not turn from me*" (Jer. 32:40). This promise recurs in many wonderful expressions in the New Testament:

- "By God's power [we] are guarded through faith for a salvation ready to be revealed in the last time." (1 Pet. 1:5)

- "Now to him who is able to keep you from stumbling and to present you blameless before the presence of his glory with great joy, to the only God, our Savior, through Jesus Christ our Lord, be glory, majesty, dominion, and authority, before all time and now and forever. Amen." (Jude 24-25)

- "May the God of peace himself sanctify you completely, and may your whole spirit and soul and body be kept blameless at the coming of our Lord Jesus Christ. He who calls you is faithful; he will surely do it." (1 Thess. 5:23-24:

- "I am sure of this, that he who began a good work in you will bring it to completion at the day of Jesus Christ." (Phil. 1:6)

- "[Jesus Christ] will sustain you to the end; guiltless in the day of our Lord Jesus Christ. God is faithful, by whom you were called into the fellowship of his Son, Jesus Christ our Lord." (1 Cor. 1:8-9)

- "Now may the God of peace who brought again from the dead our Lord Jesus, the great shepherd of the sheep, by the blood of the eternal covenant, equip you with everything good that you may do his will, working in us that which is pleasing in his sight, through Jesus Christ, to whom be glory forever and ever. Amen." (Heb. 13:20-21)

I sometimes ask people: Why do you believe you will wake up a Christian tomorrow morning? Why do you think you will have saving faith tomorrow when you wake up? I ask this to test what sort of view of perseverance someone has. The biblical answer is not: I know I will choose to believe tomorrow morning. I am committed to Jesus. That is very fragile confidence.

The answer is found in all these texts. God is faithful. God will work in me. God will keep me. God will finish his work to the end. The answer is God's ongoing work, not my ongoing commitment. When I ask this question I am fishing to see if anyone has the view that eternal security is like a vaccination. We got our vaccination when we were converted and can't catch the disease of unbelief. That is a misleading analogy because it implies that the process of preservation is automatic without the ongoing work of the great physician. Perseverance is not like a vaccination, but like a life-long therapy program in which the great physician stays with you all the way. He will never leave us (Heb. 13:5). That is the way we persevere. That is the way we have assurance.

7. Therefore we should be zealous to confirm our calling and election.

The book of 2 Peter 1:10-11 says, "Therefore, brothers, be all the more diligent to confirm your calling and election, for if you practice these qualities you will never fall. For in this way there will be richly provided for you an entrance into the eternal kingdom of our Lord and Savior Jesus Christ." Peter's point is not that our calling and election are fragile and need to be propped up. We have seen plainly, for example, from Romans 8:29-30 that calling and election are the most solid realities under God. They are links in a chain of salvation that cannot be broken.

What Peter means is: be zealous to maintain your assurance of them and to confirm them continually by walking in the joy of them. He explains in the preceding verses that God, by "his divine power has granted to us all things that pertain to life and godliness, through the knowledge of him who called us to his own glory and excellence" (2 Pet. 1:3). He has not left us to ourselves to confirm our calling and election.

By his divine power we then grow in faith and virtue and knowledge and self-control and steadfastness and godliness and brotherly affection and love (2 Pet. 1:5-7). In other words we make eager efforts to trust the promises and power of God so deeply that sin is put to death in our lives by the Spirit and the goal of love is joyfully pursued. Faith working through love (Gal. 5:6) is the way we make our calling and election sure.

8. Perseverance is a community project.

God never meant us to fight the fight of faith alone. We are to fight for each other. One of Paul's most remarkable statements about the perseverance of the elect is 2 Timothy 2:10, "I endure everything for the sake of the elect, that they also may obtain the salvation that is in Christ Jesus with eternal glory." To many this is astonishing. Isn't it already sure that the elect will obtain salvation in final glory? Yes it is. Those whom he justified he glorified.

But the question betrays an assumption that this last point is meant to remove—the assumption that certain outcomes imply that there's no need to press on toward them. That is a mistake. Salvation is certain for God's elect. It cannot fail. But the way God has ordained to make it certain is by means of empowering human partnership in the fight of faith. Paul sees his ministry of the word as essential to the perseverance of the elect.

Take a simple example. Suppose God has predestined that a nail be in a two-by-four with its head flush with the surface of the board. It is certain that this will happen. God is God and he has planned it. Does that mean he is indifferent to hammers? No. In fact God has also ordained that the way the nail will get in the board is by being struck with a hammer.

Similarly, the elect will certainly be saved in the end with eternal glory. Does that mean God is indifferent to the ministry of the world in getting them there? No. God has made it essential. And the reason that does not undermine the certainty of salvation is that God is just as sovereign over the means as he is over the ends.

We see this truth applied to all of us in Hebrews 3:12-13, "Take care, brothers, lest there be in any of you an evil, unbelieving heart, leading you to fall away from the living God. But exhort one another every day, as long as it is called 'today,' that none of you may be hardened by the deceitfulness of sin." God will not let any of his elect "fall away" into destruction. But the way he will keep us from falling (Jude 1:24) is by mutual exhortation of other believers in our lives. This is one of the highest tributes that could possibly be paid to the church. God ordains the body of Christ as the means of his infallible keeping of the elect.

We close this chapter with the hope and prayer that you will go deeper into the grace of God's persevering grace. If you linger over this truth and let it sink in, you will find that the certainty of God's covenant-keeping grace to you, is a far greater and stronger and sweeter ground of your assurance than any view of eternal security that makes it more impersonal and automatic like a vaccination. To know that God chose you, and God called you, and God gave you faith, and will never leave you, and will preserve you, and present you blameless before the presence of his glory with great joy—that assurance brings an invincible joy and strength and courage into your life. May God take you down ever deeper into the divine grace of perseverance.

8
WHAT THE FIVE POINTS HAVE MEANT FOR ME: A PERSONAL TESTIMONY

These ten points are my personal testimony to the effects of believing in the five points of Calvinism—the doctrines of grace.

1. These truths make me stand in awe of God and lead me into the depth of true God-centered worship.

I recall the time I first saw, while teaching Ephesians at Bethel College in the late 1970s, the threefold statement of the goal of all God's work, namely, "to the praise of the glory of his grace" (Eph. 1:6, 12, 14).

It has led me to see that we cannot enrich God and that therefore his glory shines most brightly not when we try to meet his needs but when we are satisfied in him as the essence of our deeds. "From him and through him and to him are all things. To him be glory forever" (Rom. 11:36). Worship becomes an end in itself.

It has made me feel how low and inadequate are my affections, so that the psalms of longing come alive and make worship intense.

2. These truths help protect me from trifling with divine things.

One of the curses of our culture is banality, cuteness, cleverness. Television is one of the main sustainers of our addiction to superficiality and triviality. God is swept into this. Hence we tend to trifle with divine things.

Earnestness is not excessive in our day. It might have been once. And, yes, there are imbalances in certain people today who don't seem to be able to relax and talk about the weather. But it seems to me that the far greater sadness in our day is people who are simply unable to be reverent. They seem to have never been awed by the greatness of God. They only know one mode of relationship: casual. This is a tragic and impoverishing incapacity.

Robertson Nicole said of Spurgeon,

> Evangelism of the humorous type [we might say, church growth of the hip, cool, clever, funny, market-savvy type] may attract multitudes, but it lays the soul in ashes and destroys the very germs of religion. Mr. Spurgeon is often thought by those who do not know his sermons to have been a humorous preacher. As a matter of fact there was no preacher whose tone was more uniformly earnest, reverent and solemn.[1]

The greatness of God that stands forth from the doctrines of grace has been a weighty ballast in my boat. It gives me great joy, and guards my heart from the plague of silliness.

3. These truths make me marvel at my own salvation.

After laying out the great, God-wrought salvation in Ephesians 1, Paul prays, in the last part of that chapter, that the effect of that theology will be the enlightenment of our hearts so that we marvel at "the hope to which he has called you ... the riches of his glorious inheritance in the saints, and ... the immeasurable greatness of his power toward us who believe" (Eph. 1:18-19). In other words, he prayed that we would experience what he had just taught. That our hearts would be able to grasp what had really happened to us.

---

1   Quoted in Iain Murray, *The Forgotten Spurgeon* (Edinburgh: Banner of Truth Trust, 1973), p. 38.

Every ground of boasting is removed. Brokenhearted joy and gratitude abound.

The piety of Jonathan Edwards begins to grow. When God has given us a taste of his own majesty and our own wickedness, then the Christian life becomes a thing very different than conventional piety. Edwards describes it beautifully when he says,

> The desires of the saints, however earnest, are humble desires: their hope is a humble hope, and their joy, even when it is unspeakable, and full of glory, is humble, brokenhearted joy, and leaves the Christian more poor in spirit, and more like a little child, and more disposed to a universal lowliness of behavior.[2]

4. These truths make me alert to man-centered substitutes that pose as good news.

In my book, *The Pleasures of God,*[3] I show that in the 18th century in New England the slide from the sovereignty of God led to Arminianism and thence to universalism and thence to Unitarianism. The same thing happened in England in the 19th century after Spurgeon.

Iain Murray's *Jonathan Edwards: A New Biography* documents the same thing: "Calvinistic convictions waned in North America. In the progress of the decline which Edwards had rightly anticipated, those Congregational churches of New England which had embraced Arminianism after the Great Awakening gradually moved into Unitarianism and universalism, led by Charles Chauncy."[4]

You can also read in J. I. Packer's *Quest for Godliness* how Richard Baxter forsook these teachings and how the following generations reaped a grim harvest in the Baxter church in Kidderminster.[5]

---

2   *Religious Affections*, New Haven: Yale University Press, 1959, pp. 339-40.

3   John Piper, *The Pleasures of God*, (Colorado Springs, CO: Multnomah Books), p. 129 in the 2012 revised edition.

4   Iain Murray, *Jonathan Edwards: A New Biography* (Edinburgh: Banner of Truth, 1987), p. 454.

5   J. I. Packer, *Quest for Godliness* (Wheaton, IL: Crossway Books, 1990), p. 160.

These doctrines are a bulwark against man-centered teachings in many forms that gradually corrupt the church and make her weak from the inside, all the while looking strong or popular. The church of the living God, rightly taught, is to be "a pillar and buttress of the truth" (1 Tim. 3:15). That is what these truths have proved to be for me.

5. These truths make me groan over the indescribable disease of our secular, God-belittling culture.

I can hardly read the newspaper or a Google news article or look at a TV ad or a billboard without feeling the burden that God is missing. When God is the main reality in the universe and is treated as a non-reality, I tremble at the wrath that is being stored up. I am still able to be shocked. Are you? Many Christians are sedated with the same God-ignoring drug as the world. Some think it is a virtue that God be neglected, and invent cynical names for people who speak of God in relation to everything. These teachings are a great antidote against that neglect and that cynicism.

Christians exist to reassert the reality of God and the supremacy of God in all of life. We are therefore in need of a great awakening. These truths keep me aware of that and impel me to pray toward it. For only a sovereign work of God can make it happen.

6. These truths make me confident that the work which God planned and began, he will finish—both globally and personally.

The truth that God will use all his sovereign power to keep me for himself is supremely precious. I know my heart. Left to itself my heart is proud and self-centered and an idol factory. Few prayers are more needful for me than this:

> O to grace how great a debtor
> Daily I'm constrained to be!
> Let Thy goodness, like a fetter,
> Bind my wandering heart to Thee.

Prone to wander, Lord, I feel it,
Prone to leave the God I love;
Here's my heart, O take and seal it,
Seal it for Thy courts above.

Yes, I need—and I want—him to chain me to himself everyday. To seal me. Capture me. Keep me. Hold on to me. And the doctrines of grace are the perfect satisfaction for these desires. This is exactly what God has promised to do for me. "I will put the fear of me in their hearts, that they may not turn from me" (Jer. 32:40). "I will uphold you with my righteous right hand" (Isa. 41:10). I go to bed at night quietly confident that I will be a secure believer in the morning not because of my free will, but because of God's free grace. This is worth more than millions of dollars.

7. **These truths make me see everything in the light of God's sovereign purposes—that from him and through him and to him are all things, to him be glory forever and ever.**
Through the lens of these doctrines I see that all of life relates to God and that he is the beginning, the middle, and the end of it all. There's no compartment where he is not all-important. He is the one who gives meaning to everything (1 Cor. 10:31).

Seeing God's sovereign purpose worked out in Scripture, and hearing Paul say that "[he] works all things according to the counsel of his will" (Eph. 1:11) make me see the world this way. Reality becomes supercharged with God. He is the all-pervading glory in all that is. Everything is from him and for him. The words of Jonathan Edwards thrill me because they represent so beautifully the implication of the doctrines of grace:

In the creature's knowing, esteeming, loving, rejoicing in, and praising God, the glory of God is both *exhibited* and *acknowledged*; his fullness is *received* and *returned*. Here is both an *emanation* and *remanation*. The refulgence shines upon and into the creature, and is reflected back to the luminary. The beams of glory come from God, are something of God, and are refunded back again to their original. So that the whole is *of* God, and *in* God, and *to* God; and he is the beginning, and the middle, and the end.[6]

8. These truths make me hopeful that God has the will, the right, and the power to answer prayer that people be changed.

The warrant for prayer is that God may break in and change things—including the human heart. He can turn the will around. "Hallowed be your name" (Matt. 6:9) means: cause people who are not hallowing your name to hallow your name. "May your word run and be glorified" (2 Thess. 3:1) means: cause hearts to be opened to the gospel. This is what God did for me in answer to my parents' prayers. It is what I now gladly do for others.

I take the new covenant promises and plead with God to bring them to pass in people's lives and among all the mission frontiers of the world. And the reason I pray this way is that God has the right and the power to do these things. No human autonomy stands in the way.

"God, take out of their flesh their heart of stone and give them a new heart of flesh." (Ezek. 11:19)

"Lord, circumcise their hearts so that they love you." (Deut. 30:6)

"Father, put your spirit within them and cause them to walk in your statutes." (Ezek. 36:27)

"Lord, grant them repentance and the knowledge of the truth that they may escape from the snare of the devil." (2 Tim. 2:25-26)

---

6   Jonathan Edwards, *The End for Which God Created the World*, p. 275, in John Piper's, *God's Passion for His Glory*, (Wheaton, Illinois: Crossway Books, 1998), p. 248.

"Father, open their hearts so that they believe the gospel."
(Acts 16:14)

Prayer is where most Christians sound like Calvinists. Most sincere Christians pray with the assumption that he has the right and power not only to heal human bodies and alter natural circumstances, but also to sovereignly transform human hearts. In other words prayer is based on God's ability to overcome human resistance. That is what we ask him to do. Which means that the doctrine of irresistible grace is the great hope of answered prayer in the lives of people for whose salvation I plead.

9. These truths remind me that evangelism is absolutely essential for people to come to Christ and be saved, and that there is great hope for success in leading people to faith, but that conversion is not finally dependent on me or limited by the hardness of the unbeliever.

The doctrines of grace make evangelism among spiritually dead sinners possible. Without the sovereign grace of God we may as well be preaching in a cemetery. Because we *are* preaching in a cemetery. That is what this world is. The truth of total depravity means that the preaching of the cross is foolishness to the natural man, and "he is not able to understand them because they are spiritually discerned" (1 Cor. 2:14). So evangelism only makes sense in the light of the doctrines of grace. We really believe God can raise the dead.

And we know he uses the human means to do it. "You have been born again, not of perishable seed but of imperishable, *through the living and abiding word of God*" (1 Pet. 1:23). The sovereign work of God in giving new life to the dead human heart is "through the word of God." And Peter adds, "This word is the good news that was preached to you" (1 Pet. 1:25). It's the gospel. This is the power of God unto salvation (Rom. 1:16).

Therefore the doctrines of grace give hope for evangelism in the hardest places. Dead is dead. Muslims or Hindus or hardened European post-Christian secularists are not more dead than any other "natural man." And God does the impossible. He raises the dead (Eph. 2:1-6). When faced with the hardheartedness of the rich young ruler Jesus said, "With man this is impossible, but with God all things are possible" (Matt. 19:26).

As I look out on the remaining task of world missions I do not despair. Rather I hear Jesus say, "I have other sheep that are not of this fold. I must bring them also and they will listen to my voice" (John 10:16). Not: they may. But: they *will*. So I say: this cannot fail. The doctrines of grace enflamed world missions in the lives of William Carey and David Livingston and Adoniram Judson and Henry Martyn and John Paton and thousands of others. And that is the effect it has had on me, as I have tried to do my part in promoting the great work of frontier missions.

10. These truths make me sure that God will triumph in the end.
"I am God, and there is no other; I am God, and there is none like me, declaring the end from the beginning and from ancient times things not yet done, saying, 'My counsel shall stand, and I will accomplish all my purpose'" (Isa. 46:9-10).

The sum of the matter is that God is God. He is absolutely sovereign. And he is gracious beyond all human analogy. He has not left the world to perish in its sin. He has planned, is performing, and will complete a great salvation for his people and his creation. He has done this with infinite wisdom and love. Which means he has done it so that he gets the glory in us and we get the joy in him. And it cannot fail. "The counsel of the Lord stands forever" (Ps. 33:11).

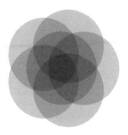

9
CONCLUDING TESTIMONIES

The aim of this book has been to persuade the mind concerning biblical truth and thus awaken a deeper experience of God's sovereign grace. I am ever aware of the terrible sentence, "Even the demons believe—and shudder!" (James 2:19). In other words, it is possible to be persuaded of a reality at one level and have no sweet experience of that reality at another level. Jonathan Edwards said there are two ways to know whether the sticky brown material in the bowl is sweet. You can deduce from color and smell and particles of honeycomb that this is honey and then know by inference that it is sweet because honey is sweet. Or you can taste it. My prayer is that the sweetness of God's sovereign grace will not merely be inferred, but also tasted.

I hope you will have the sweet experience of resting in the massive comfort of these truths. I want you to feel the tremendous incentive for love and righteousness and for risk-taking missions flowing from these truths. And I pray that your experience knowing and trusting the sovereign grace of God will be such that God gets great glory in your life.

To this end, I have gathered here some testimonies of what these truths have meant to some great Christians of the past. For those who have known the doctrines of grace truly, they have never been mere speculation for the head, but have always been power for the heart and life.

Augustine of Hippo (354–430)

A thousand years before the Reformation, Augustine savored the sovereignty of grace in his own life. He was resoundingly converted by the irresistible grace of God after leading a dissolute life. He wrote in his *Confessions* (X, 40):

> I have no hope at all but in thy great mercy. Grant what thou commandest and command what thou wilt. Thou dost enjoin on us continence. ... Truly by continence are we bound together and brought back into that unity from which we were dissipated into a plurality. For he loves thee too little who loves anything together with thee, which he loves not for thy sake. O love that ever burnest and art never quenched! O Charity, my God, enkindle me! Thou commandest continence. Grant what thou commandest and command what thou wilt.[1]

These are the words of a man who loves the truth of irresistible grace, because he knows he is utterly undone without it. But also in his doctrinal letters, he drives this beloved truth home (*Epistle ccxvii*, to Vitalis):

> If, as I prefer to think in your case, you agree with us in supposing that we are doing our duty in praying to God, as our custom is, for them that refuse to believe, that they may be willing to believe and for those who resist and oppose his law and doctrine, that they may believe and follow it. If you agree with us in thinking that we are doing our duty in giving thanks to God, as is our custom, for such people when they have

---

1   Quoted in *Documents of the Christian Church*, ed. by Henry Bettenson [London: Oxford University Press, 1967], p. 54.

been converted. ... then you are surely bound to admit that the wills of men are preveniently moved by the grace of God, and that it is God who makes them to will the good which they refused; for it is God whom we ask so to do, and we know that it is meet and right to give thanks to him for so doing.

For Augustine, the truth of irresistible grace was the foundation of his prayers for the conversion of the lost and of his thanks to God when they were converted.

Jonathan Edwards (1703–1758)

Jonathan Edwards, the great New England preacher and theologian, had an equally deep love for these truths. He wrote when he was 26 about the day he fell in love with the sovereignty of God:

There has been a wonderful alteration in my mind, in respect to the doctrine of God's sovereignty, from that day to this. ... God's absolute sovereignty ... is what my mind seems to rest assured of, as much as of any thing that I see with my eyes. ... The doctrine has very often appeared exceeding pleasant, bright, and sweet. Absolute sovereignty is what I love to ascribe to God ... God's sovereignty has ever appeared to me, a great part of his glory. It has often been my delight to approach God, and adore him as a sovereign God.[2]

George Whitefield (1714–1770)

Edwards wept openly when George Whitefield preached in his church, because of how much he loved the message he preached. Whitefield was a great evangelist and said, "I embrace the Calvinistic scheme, not because Calvin, but Jesus Christ has taught it to me."[3]

---

2   "Personal Narrative," quoted in *Jonathan Edwards, Selections* [New York: Hill & Wang, 1935], p. 59.

3   Arnold Dallimore, *George Whitefield*, Vol. 1 (Edinburgh: Banner of Truth Trust, 1970), p. 406.

He pleaded with John Wesley not to oppose the doctrines of Calvinism:

> I cannot bear the thoughts of opposing you: but how can I avoid it, if you go about (as your brother Charles once said) to drive John Calvin out of Bristol. Alas, I never read anything that Calvin wrote; my doctrines I had from Christ and His apostles; I was taught them of God.[4]

It was these beliefs that filled him with holy zeal for evangelism:

> The doctrines of our election, and free justification in Christ Jesus are daily more and more pressed upon my heart. They fill my soul with a holy fire and afford me great confidence in God my Saviour.
>
> I hope we shall catch fire from each other, and that there will be a holy emulation amongst us, who shall most debase man and exalt the Lord Jesus. Nothing but the doctrines of the Reformation can do this. All others leave free will in man and make him, in part at least, a saviour to himself. My soul, come not thou near the secret of those who teach such things. ... I know Christ is all in all. Man is nothing: he hath a free will to go to hell, but none to go to heaven, till God worketh in him to will and to do his good pleasure.
>
> Oh, the excellency of the doctrine of election and of the saints' final perseverance! I am persuaded, til a man comes to believe and feel these important truths, he cannot come out of himself, but when convinced of these and assured of their application to his own heart, he then walks by faith indeed![5]

---

4   Ibid., p. 574.

5   Ibid., p. 407.

George Mueller (1805–1898)

George Mueller is famous for the orphanages he founded and the amazing faith he had to pray for God's provision. Not many people know the theology that undergirded that great ministry. In his mid-twenties (1829), he had an experience which he records later as follows:

> Before this period [when I came to prize the Bible alone as my standard of judgment] I had been much opposed to the doctrines of election, particular redemption (limited atonement), and final persevering grace. But now I was brought to examine these precious truths by the Word of God. Being made willing to have no glory of my own in the conversion of sinners, but to consider myself merely an instrument; and being made willing to receive what the Scriptures said, I went to the Word, reading the New Testament from the beginning, with a particular reference to these truths.

> To my great astonishment I found that the passages which speak decidedly for election and persevering grace, were about four times as many as those which speak apparently against these truths; and even those few, shortly after, when I had examined and understood them, served to confirm me in the above doctrines.

> As to the effect which my belief in these doctrines had on me, I am constrained to state for God's glory, that though I am still exceedingly weak, and by no means so dead to the lusts of the flesh, and the lust of the eyes, and the pride of life, as I might be, and as I ought to be, yet, by the grace of God, I have walked more closely with Him since that period. My life has not been so variable, and I may say that I have lived much more for God than before.[6]

---

6   *Autobiography* (London: J. Nisbet & Co., 1906), pp. 33-34.

Charles Spurgeon (1834–1892)

C. H. Spurgeon was a contemporary of George Mueller. He was the pastor of the Metropolitan Tabernacle in London and the most famous pastor of his day—and a Baptist at that. His preaching was powerful to the winning of souls to Christ. But what was his gospel that held thousands spellbound each week and brought many to the Savior?

> I have my own private opinion that there is no such thing as preaching Christ and him crucified, unless we preach what is nowadays called Calvinism. It is a nickname to call it Calvinism; Calvinism is the gospel, and nothing else. I do not believe we can preach the gospel ... unless we preach the sovereignty of God in His dispensation of grace; nor unless we exalt the electing, unchangeable, eternal, immutable, conquering love of Jehovah; nor do I think we can preach the gospel unless we base it upon the special and particular redemption (limited atonement) of His elect and chosen people which Christ wrought out upon the Cross; nor can I comprehend a gospel which lets saints fall away after they are called.[7]

He had not always believed these things. Spurgeon recounts his discovery of these truths at the age of 16:

> Born, as all of us are by nature, an Arminian, I still believed the old things I had heard continually from the pulpit, and did not see the grace of God. When I was coming to Christ, I thought I was doing it all myself, and though I sought the Lord earnestly, I had no idea the Lord was seeking me. ... I can recall the very day and hour when first I received those

---

7   *Autobiography*, Vol. 1 (Edinburgh: Banner of Truth Trust, 1962, orig. 1897), p. 168.

truths in my own soul—when they were, as John Bunyan says, burnt into my heart as with a hot iron. ...

One week-night, when I was sitting in the house of God, I was not thinking much about the preacher's sermon, for I did not believe it. The thought struck me, "How did you come to be a Christian?" I sought the Lord. "But how did you come to seek the Lord?" The truth flashed across my mind in a moment—I should not have sought Him unless there had been some previous influence in my mind to make me seek Him. I prayed, thought I, but then I asked myself, How came I to pray? I was induced to pray by reading the Scriptures. How came I to read the Scriptures? I did read them, but what led me to do so? Then, in a moment, I saw that God was at the bottom of it all, and that He was the Author of my faith, and so the whole doctrine of grace opened up to me, and from that doctrine I have not departed to this day, and I desire to make this my constant confession, "I ascribe my change wholly to God."[8]

Spurgeon started a college for pastors and was intent that the key to being a worthy teacher in the church was to grasp these doctrines of grace.

Arminianism is thus guilty of confusing doctrines and of acting as an obstruction to a clear and lucid grasp of the Scripture; because it misstates or ignores the eternal purpose of God, it dislocates the meaning of the whole plan of redemption. Indeed confusion is inevitable apart from this foundational truth [of election].

Without it there is a lack of unity of thought, and generally speaking they have no idea whatever of a system of divinity.

8   Ibid., pp. 164-165.

It is almost impossible to make a man a theologian unless you begin with this [doctrine of election].

You may if you please put a young believer to college for years, but unless you shew him this ground-plan of the everlasting covenant, he will make little progress, because his studies do not cohere, he does not see how one truth fits with another, and how all truths must harmonize together...

Take any county throughout England, you will find poor men hedging and ditching that have a better knowledge of divinity than one half of those who come from our academies and colleges, for the reason simply and entirely that these men have first learned in their youth the system of which election is a centre, and have afterwards found their own experience exactly squares with it.[9]

---

9   Charles Spurgeon, "Effects Of Sound Doctrine," sermon delivered on Sunday evening, April 22, 1860, at New Park Street Chapel.

10
A FINAL APPEAL

It is fitting that we close this short book on the doctrines of grace by appealing to you, the reader, to receive the magnificent Christ who is the eternal Author of these doctrines. Give heed to the beautiful entreaty extended by J. I. Packer, a great contemporary advocate of these truths:

> To the question: what must I do to be saved? the old gospel [Calvinism] replies: believe on the Lord Jesus Christ. To the further question: what does it mean to believe on the Lord Jesus Christ? its reply is: it means knowing oneself to be a sinner, and Christ to have died for sinners; abandoning all self-righteousness and self-confidence, and casting oneself wholly upon Him for pardon and peace; and exchanging one's natural enmity and rebellion against God for a spirit of grateful submission to the will of Christ through the renewing of one's heart by the Holy Ghost.

> And to the further question still: how am I to go about believing on Christ and repenting, if I have no natural ability to do these things? it answers: look to Christ, speak to Christ, cry to Christ, just as you are; confess your sin, your impenitence,

your unbelief, and cast yourself on His mercy; ask Him to give you a new heart, working in you true repentance and firm faith; ask Him to take away your evil heart of unbelief and to write His law within you, that you may never henceforth stray from Him. Turn to Him and trust Him as best you can, and pray for grace to turn and trust more thoroughly; use the means of grace expectantly, looking to Christ to draw near to you as you seek to draw near to Him; watch, pray, read, and hear God's Word, worship and commune with God's people, and so continue till you know in yourself beyond doubt that you are indeed a changed being, a penitent believer, and the new heart which you desired has been put within you.[1]

Let Charles Spurgeon lead you in prayer:

Join with me in prayer at this moment, I entreat you. Join with me while I put words into your mouths, and speak them on your behalf—"Lord, I am guilty, I deserve thy wrath. Lord, I cannot save myself. Lord, I would have a new heart and a right spirit, but what can I do? Lord, I can do nothing, come and work in me to will and to do thy good pleasure.

Thou alone hast power, I know,
To save a wretch like me;
To whom, or whither should I go
If I should run from thee?

But I now do from my very soul call upon thy name. Trembling, yet believing, I cast myself wholly upon thee, O Lord, I trust the blood and righteousness of thy dear Son .... Lord, save me tonight, for Jesus' sake."[2]

---

1   J. I. Packer, *The Quest for Godliness* (Wheaton: Crossway, 1994), p. 144.

2   Quoted in Iain Murray, *The Forgotten Spurgeon* (Edinburgh: Banner of Truth Trust, 1973), pp. 101-102.

desiringGod

If you would like to explore further the vision of God and life presented in this book, we at Desiring God would love to serve you. We have thousands of resources to help you grow in your passion for Jesus Christ and help you spread that passion to others. At desiringGod.org, you'll find almost everything John Piper has written and preached, including more than sixty books. We've made over thirty years of his sermons available free online for you to read, listen to, download, and watch.

In addition, you can access hundreds of articles, find out where John Piper is speaking, and learn about our conferences. Desiring God has a whatever-you-can-afford policy, designed for individuals with limited discretionary funds. If you'd like more information about this policy, please contact us at the address or phone number below. We exist to help you treasure Jesus and his gospel above all things because *he is most glorified in you when you are most satisfied in him*. Let us know how we can serve you!

Desiring God

Post Office Box 2901 / Minneapolis, Minnesota 55402
888.346.4700 mail@desiringGod.org

Christian Focus Publications

Our mission statement –

STAYING FAITHFUL

In dependence upon God we seek to impact the world through literature faithful to His infallible Word, the Bible. Our aim is to ensure that the Lord Jesus Christ is presented as the only hope to obtain forgiveness of sin, live a useful life and look forward to heaven with Him.

Our Books are published in four imprints:

CHRISTIAN
FOCUS

popular works including biographies, commentaries, basic doctrine and Christian living.

CHRISTIAN
HERITAGE

books representing some of the best material from the rich heritage of the church.

MENTOR

books written at a level suitable for Bible College and seminary students, pastors, and other serious readers. The imprint includes commentaries, doctrinal studies, examination of current issues and church history.

CF4•K

children's books for quality Bible teaching and for all age groups: Sunday school curriculum, puzzle and activity books; personal and family devotional titles, biographies and inspirational stories – Because you are never too young to know Jesus!

Christian Focus Publications Ltd,
Geanies House, Fearn, Ross-shire,
IV20 1TW, Scotland, United Kingdom.
www.christianfocus.com
blog.christianfocus.com